TO:

FROM:

A SPECIAL MESSAGE:

THIS WAY

FOLLOWING HIM EVERY DAY:

100 Essential Devos For Tweens

The quoted ideas expressed in this book (but not Scripture verses) are not, in all cases, exact quotations, as some have been edited for clarity and brevity. In all cases, the author has attempted to maintain the speaker's original intent. In some cases, quoted material for this book was obtained from secondary sources, primarily print media. While every effort was made to ensure the accuracy of these sources, the accuracy cannot be guaranteed. For additions, deletions, corrections, or clarifications in future editions of this text, please write Freeman-Smith.

Scripture quotations are taken from:

The Holy Bible, King James Version (KJV)

The Holy Bible, New International Version (NIV) Copyright © 1973, 1978, 1984, by International Bible Society. Used by permission of Zondervan Publishing House. All rights reserved.

The Holy Bible, New King James Version (NKJV) Copyright © 1982 by Thomas Nelson, Inc. Used by permission.

Holy Bible, New Living Translation, (NLT) copyright © 1996. Used by permission of Tyndale House Publishers, Inc., Wheaton, Illinois 60189. All rights reserved.

The Message (MSG)- This edition issued by contractual arrangement with NavPress, a division of The Navigators, U.S.A. Originally published by NavPress in English as THE MESSAGE: The Bible in Contemporary Language copyright 2002-2003 by Eugene Peterson. All rights reserved.

New Century Version®. (NCV) Copyright © 1987, 1988, 1991 by Word Publishing, a division of Thomas Nelson, Inc. All rights reserved. Used by permission.

The New American Standard Bible®, (NASB) Copyright © 1960, 1962, 1963, 1968, 1971, 1972, 1973, 1975, 1977, 1995 by The Lockman Foundation. Used by permission.

International Children's Bible®, New Century Version®. (ICB) Copyright © 1986, 1988, 1999 by Tommy Nelson™, a division of Thomas Nelson, Inc. All rights reserved. Used by permission.

The Holy Bible, The Living Bible (TLB), Copyright © 1971 owned by assignment by Illinois Regional Bank N.A. (as trustee). Used by permission of Tyndale House Publishers, Inc., Wheaton, Illinois 60189. All rights reserved.

The Holman Christian Standard Bible™ (HCSB) Copyright © 1999, 2000, 2001 by Holman Bible Publishers. Used by permission.

Cover Design by Kim Russell / Wahoo Designs
Page Layout by Bart Dawson

ISBN 978-1-60587-362-6

THIS WAY

Hi!

ENTER
EXIT

here

FOLLOWING
HIM
EVERY DAY:

100 Essential Devos For Tweens

IN

OUT

FOLLOW

NEXT

LOOK

THIS WAY

INTRODUCTION

What's the most important decision you'll ever make? That's easy: it's the decision to follow Jesus. And, the sooner you learn to follow Him, the better.

Every life—including yours—is a series of wins and losses, celebrations and disappointments, triumphs and troubles. Every step of the way, through all the ups and downs, Jesus will guide you and protect you if you let Him. Your job, of course, is to let Him. And, the ideas in this book can help.

Would you like to build a stronger faith and better future? Then, make up your mind to follow Jesus every day. When you do, you won't just change the direction of your day . . . you'll also change the direction of your life right now and forever.

NEXT

FOLLOW HIM
EVERY DAY

"Follow Me," Jesus told them, "and I will make you into fishers of men!" Immediately they left their nets and followed Him.

Mark 1:17-18 HCSB

Can you honestly say that you're serious about your faith and that you're really following Jesus? Hopefully so. But if you're preoccupied with other things—or if you're strictly a one-day-a-week Christian—then you're in need of a major-league spiritual makeover.

Jesus doesn't want you to be a lukewarm believer; Jesus wants you to be a "new creation" through Him. And that's exactly what you should want for yourself, too. Nothing is more important than your wholehearted commitment to your Creator and to His only begotten Son. Your faith must never be an afterthought; it must be your ultimate priority, your ultimate possession, and your ultimate passion.

You are the recipient of Christ's love. Accept it enthusiastically and share it passionately. Jesus deserves your undivided attention. And when you give it to Him, you'll be forever grateful that you did.

MORE FROM GOD'S WORD

Then he told them what they could expect for themselves: "Anyone who intends to come with me has to let me lead."

Luke 9:23 MSG

Whoever is not willing to carry the cross and follow me is not worthy of me. Those who try to hold on to their lives will give up true life. Those who give up their lives for me will hold on to true life.

Matthew 10:38-39 NCV

If anyone would come after me, he must deny himself and take up his cross and follow me.

Mark 8:34 NIV

10

SOME BIG IDEAS

Christ is like a river that is continually flowing. There are always fresh supplies of water coming from the fountain-head, so that a man may live by it and be supplied with water all his life. So Christ is an ever-flowing fountain; he is continually supplying his people, and the fountain is not spent. They who live upon Christ may have fresh supplies from him for all eternity; they may have an increase of blessedness that is new, and new still, and which never will come to an end.

Jonathan Edwards

Jesus challenges you and me to keep our focus daily on the cross of His will if we want to be His disciples.

Anne Graham Lotz

> Remember that God blesses those who choose to follow Christ. Jesus is ready to lead you; it's up to you to follow.

It's your heart that Jesus longs for: your will to be made His own with self on the cross forever, and Jesus alone on the throne.

Ruth Bell Graham

11

WORSHIP GOD EVERY DAY

Worship the Lord your God and . . . serve Him only.

Matthew 4:10 HCSB

If you really want to know God, you must be willing to worship Him seven days a week, not just on Sunday.

God has a wonderful plan for your life, and an important part of that plan includes the time that you set aside for praise and worship. Every life, including yours, is based upon some form of worship. The question is not whether you will worship, but what you worship.

If you choose to worship God, you will receive a bountiful harvest of joy, peace, and abundance. But if you distance yourself from God by foolishly worshiping earthly possessions and personal gratification, you're making a huge mistake. So do this: Worship God today and every day. Worship Him with sincerity and thanksgiving. Write His name on your heart and rest assured that He, too, has written your name on His.

MORE FROM GOD'S WORD

I rejoiced with those who said to me, "Let us go to the house of the Lord."

Psalm 122:1 HCSB

And every day they devoted themselves to meeting together in the temple complex, and broke bread from house to house. They ate their food with gladness and simplicity of heart, praising God and having favor with all the people. And every day the Lord added those being saved to them.

Acts 2:46-47 HCSB

But an hour is coming, and is now here, when the true worshipers will worship the Father in spirit and truth. Yes, the Father wants such people to worship Him. God is Spirit, and those who worship Him must worship in spirit and truth."

John 4:23-24 HCSB

So that at the name of Jesus every knee should bow—of those who are in heaven and on earth and under the earth—and every tongue should confess that Jesus Christ is Lord, to the glory of God the Father.

Philippians 2:10-11 HCSB

SOME BIG IDEAS

Worship is a voluntary act of gratitude offered by the saved to the Savior, by the healed to the Healer, by the delivered to the Deliverer.

Max Lucado

Worship is spiritual. Our worship must be more than just outward expression, it must also take place in our spirits.

Franklin Graham

Worship is not meant to be boxed up in a church building on Sunday morning. To the contrary, praise and worship should be woven into the very fabric of your life.

Worship and worry cannot live in the same heart; they are mutually exclusive.

Ruth Bell Graham

To worship Him in truth means to worship Him honestly, without hypocrisy, standing open and transparent before Him.

Anne Graham Lotz

YOU CAN MOVE MOUNTAINS

For I assure you: If you have faith the size of a mustard seed, you will tell this mountain, "Move from here to there," and it will move. Nothing will be impossible for you.

Matthew 17:20 HCSB

Because we live in a demanding world, all of us have mountains to climb and mountains to move. Moving those mountains requires faith.

Are you a mountain-moving Christian whose faith is evident for all to see? Or, are you a spiritual under-achiever? As you think about the answer to that question, consider this: God needs more people who are willing to move mountains for His glory and for His kingdom.

Are you willing to let God help you move mountains, or are you still stumbling around over a few little molehills? The answer should be obvious. And so, with no more delays, let the mountain moving begin.

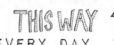

MORE FROM GOD'S WORD

Be on the alert, stand firm in the faith, act like men, be strong.

1 Corinthians 16:13 NASB

For whatever is born of God overcomes the world. And this is the victory that has overcome the world—our faith.

1 John 5:4 NKJV

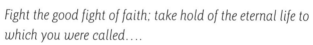

Fight the good fight of faith; take hold of the eternal life to which you were called....

1 Timothy 6:12 NASB

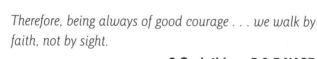

Therefore, being always of good courage . . . we walk by faith, not by sight.

2 Corinthians 5:6-7 NASB

SOME BIG IDEAS

A faith that hasn't been tested can't be trusted.

Adrian Rogers

Faith never knows where it is being led, but it loves and knows the One Who is leading.

Oswald Chambers

Great hopes make great men.

Thomas Fuller

We are never stronger than the moment we admit we are weak.

Beth Moore

Faith is stronger than fear.
John Maxwell

17

THE ULTIMATE TRUTH

You will know the truth, and the truth will set you free.
John 8:32 HCSB

God is vitally concerned with truth. His Word teaches the truth; His Spirit reveals the truth; His Son leads us to the truth. When we open our hearts to God, and when we allow His Son to rule over our thoughts and our lives, God reveals Himself, and we come to understand the truth about ourselves and the Truth (with a capital T) about God's gift of grace.

The familiar words of John 8:32 remind us that when we come to know God's Truth, we are liberated. Have you been liberated by that Truth? And are you living in accordance with the eternal truths that you find in God's Holy Word? Hopefully so.

Today, as you fulfill the responsibilities that God has placed before you, ask yourself this question: "Do my thoughts and actions bear witness to the ultimate Truth that God has placed in my heart, or am I allowing the pressures of everyday life to overwhelm me?" It's a profound question that deserves an answer . . . now.

MORE FROM GOD'S WORD

Be diligent to present yourself approved to God, a worker who doesn't need to be ashamed, correctly teaching the word of truth.

2 Timothy 2:15 HCSB

These are the things you must do: Speak truth to one another; render honest and peaceful judgments in your gates.

Zechariah 8:16 HCSB

For God's wrath is revealed from heaven against all godlessness and unrighteousness of people who by their unrighteousness suppress the truth.

Romans 1:18 HCSB

You have already heard about this hope in the message of truth, the gospel that has come to you. It is bearing fruit and growing all over the world, just as it has among you since the day you heard it and recognized God's grace in the truth.

Colossians 1:5-6 HCSB

SOME BIG IDEAS

Let everything perish! Dismiss these empty vanities! And let us take up the search for the truth.

St. Augustine

We must go out and live among them, manifesting the gentle, loving spirit of our Lord. We need to make friends before we can hope to make converts.

Lottie Moon

It's not enough to hear God's truth, or even to understand it. If you're serious about your faith, you must allow yourself to be transformed by God's truth.

The Christian faith is meant to be lived moment by moment. It isn't some broad, general outline—it's a long walk with a real Person. Details count: passing thoughts, small sacrifices, a few encouraging words, little acts of kindness, brief victories over nagging sins.

Joni Eareckson Tada

HE'S HERE

I am not alone, because the Father is with Me.

John 16:32 HCSB

D o you ever wonder if God really hears your prayers? If so, you're in good company: lots of very faithful Christians have wondered the same thing. In fact, some of the biggest heroes in the Bible had their doubts—and so, perhaps, will you. But when you have your doubts, remember this: God isn't on vacation, and He hasn't moved out of town. God isn't taking a coffee break, and He isn't snoozing on the couch. He's right here, right now, listening to your thoughts and prayers, watching over your every move.

As the demands of everyday life weigh down upon you, you may be tempted to ignore God's presence or—worse yet—to rebel against His commandments. But, when you quiet yourself and acknowledge His presence, God touches your heart and restores your spirits. So why not let Him do it right now?

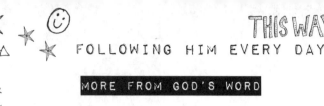

MORE FROM GOD'S WORD

Come near to God, and God will come near to you. You sinners, clean sin out of your lives. You who are trying to follow God and the world at the same time, make your thinking pure.

James 4:8 NCV

For the eyes of the Lord range throughout the earth to strengthen those whose hearts are fully committed to him.

2 Chronicles 16:9 NIV

Fear not, for I am with you; Be not dismayed, for I am your God. I will strengthen you.

Isaiah 41:10 NKJV

The eyes of the Lord are in every place, keeping watch . . . .

Proverbs 15:3 NKJV

SOME BIG IDEAS

Get yourself into the presence of the loving Father. Just place yourself before Him, and look up into, His face; think of His love, His wonderful, tender, pitying love.

Andrew Murray

There is a basic urge: the longing for unity. You desire a reunion with God—with God your Father.

E. Stanley Jones

God walks with us. He scoops us up in His arms or simply sits with us in silent strength until we cannot avoid the awesome recognition that yes, even now, He is here.

Gloria Gaither

> If you're here, God is here. If you're there, God is, too. You can't get away from Him or His love . . . thank goodness!

GOD OFFERS ETERNAL LIFE

For God loved the world in this way: He gave His only Son, so that everyone who believes in Him will not perish but have eternal life.

John 3:16 HCSB

Your decision to allow Christ to reign over your heart is the pivotal decision of your life. It is a decision that you cannot ignore. It is a decision that is yours and yours alone.

God's love for you is deeper and more profound than you can imagine. God's love for you is so great that He sent His only Son to this earth to die for your sins and to offer you the priceless gift of eternal life. Now, you must decide whether or not to accept God's gift. Will you ignore it or embrace it? Will you accept Christ's love and build a lifelong relationship with Him, or will you turn away from Him and take a different path? Accept God's gift now: allow His Son to preside over your heart, your thoughts, and your life, starting this very instant.

MORE FROM GOD'S WORD

Yet we know that no one is justified by the works of the law but by faith in Jesus Christ. And we have believed in Christ Jesus, so that we might be justified by faith in Christ and not by the works of the law, because by the works of the law no human being will be justified.

Galatians 2:16 HCSB

Whoever believes that Jesus is the Christ is born of God, and everyone who loves Him who begot also loves him who is begotten of Him.

1 John 5:1 NKJV

God wanted to make known to those among the Gentiles the glorious wealth of this mystery, which is Christ in you, the hope of glory.

Colossians 1:27 HCSB

And we have seen and testify that the Father has sent the Son as Savior of the world.

1 John 4:14 NKJV

NEXT

SOME BIG IDEAS

Evidence of new birth is that we see the rule of God.

Oswald Chambers

It's your heart that Jesus longs for: your will to be made His own with self on the cross forever, and Jesus alone on the throne.

Ruth Bell Graham

It is critically important to be certain that you have welcomed Christ into your heart. If you've accepted Christ, way to go! If not, the time to accept Him is now!

The amount of power you experience to live a victorious, triumphant Christian life is directly proportional to the freedom you give the Spirit to be Lord of your life!

Anne Graham Lotz

Choose Jesus Christ! Deny yourself, take up the Cross, and follow Him— for the world must be shown. The world must see, in us, a discernible, visible, startling difference.

Elisabeth Elliot

LOOK FOR MIRACLES

God verified the message by signs and wonders and various miracles and by giving gifts of the Holy Spirit whenever he chose to do so.

Hebrews 2:4 NLT

One way we can strengthen our faith is by looking carefully at the miraculous things that God does. But sometimes, we're simply too preoccupied to notice. Instead of paying careful attention to God's handiwork, we become distracted. Instead of expecting God to work miracles, we become cynical. Instead of depending on God's awesome power, we seek to muddle along using our own power—with decidedly mixed results.

If you lack the faith that God can work miracles in your own life, it's time to reconsider. Instead of doubting God, trust His power, and expect His miracles. Then, wait patiently . . . because something miraculous is about to happen.

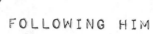 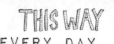
MORE FROM GOD'S WORD

Looking at them, Jesus said, "With men it is impossible, but not with God, because all things are possible with God."

Mark 10:27 HCSB

But as it is written: "Eye has not seen, nor ear heard, nor have entered into the heart of man the things which God has prepared for those who love Him."

1 Corinthians 2:9 NKJV

I assure you: The one who believes in Me will also do the works that I do. And he will do even greater works than these, because I am going to the Father.

John 14:12 HCSB

For nothing will be impossible with God.

Luke 1:37 HCSB

SOME BIG IDEAS

Only God can move mountains, but faith and prayer can move God.

E. M. Bounds

When God is involved, anything can happen. Be open and stay that way. God has a beautiful way of bringing good vibrations out of broken chords.

Charles Swindoll

I could go through this day oblivious to the miracles all around me or I could tune in and "enjoy."

Gloria Gaither

The healing acts of Jesus were themselves a message that he had come to set men free.

Francis MacNutt

God has infinite power. If you're watchful, you'll observe many miracles. So keep your eyes, your heart, and your mind open.

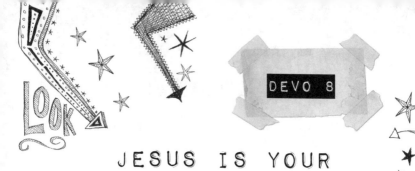

JESUS IS YOUR BEST FRIEND

Therefore if any man be in Christ, he is a new creature: old things are passed away; behold, all things are become new.

2 Corinthians 5:17 KJV

Our circumstances change but Jesus does not. Even when the world seems to be trembling between our feet, Jesus remains the spiritual bedrock that cannot be moved.

The old familiar hymn begins, "What a friend we have in Jesus . . . ." No truer words were ever penned. Jesus is the sovereign Friend and ultimate Savior of mankind. Christ showed enduring love for His believers by willingly sacrificing His own life so that we might have eternal life. Let us love Him, praise Him, and share His message of salvation with our neighbors and with the world.

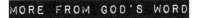
MORE FROM GOD'S WORD

And Jesus said to them, "I am the bread of life. He who comes to Me shall never hunger, and he who believes in Me shall never thirst."

John 6:35 NKJV

At the name of Jesus every knee should bow, of those in heaven, and of those on earth, and of those under the earth, and that every tongue should confess that Jesus Christ is Lord, to the glory of God the Father.

Philippians 2:10-11 NKJV

For I am persuaded, that neither death, nor life, nor angels, nor principalities, nor powers, nor things present, nor things to come, nor height, nor depth, nor any other creature, shall be able to separate us from the love of God, which is in Christ Jesus our Lord.

Romans 8:38-39 KJV

For the Son of Man has come to save that which was lost.

Matthew 18:11 NKJV

NEXT

SOME BIG IDEAS

Jesus was the perfect reflection of God's nature in every situation He encountered during His time here on earth.

Bill Hybels

Jesus: the proof of God's love.

Philip Yancey

> The Truth with a Capital "T": Jesus is the Truth, and that's the truth!

Abide in Jesus, the sinless one—which means, give up all of self and its life, and dwell in God's will and rest in His strength. This is what brings the power that does not commit sin.

Andrew Murray

Our responsibility is to feed from Him, to stay close to Him, to follow Him—because sheep easily go astray—so that we eternally experience the protection and companionship of our Great Shepherd the Lord Jesus Christ.

Franklin Graham

CELEBRATE LIFE

This is the day the Lord has made; let us rejoice and be glad in it.

Psalm 118:24 HCSB

Do you want to know God more intimately? Try this: celebrate the life He has given you.

Do you feel like celebrating today? If you're a believer, you should. When you allow Christ to reign over your heart, today and every day should be a time for joyful celebration.

What do you expect from the day ahead? Are you expecting God to do wonderful things, or are you living beneath a cloud of worry and doubt? The words of Psalm 118:24 remind us that every day is a gift from God. So whatever this day holds for you, begin it and end it with God as your partner and Christ as your Savior. And throughout the day, give thanks to the One who created you and saved you. God's love for you is infinite. Accept it; celebrate it; and be thankful.

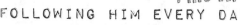
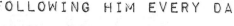
MORE FROM GOD'S WORD

Celebrate God all day, every day. I mean, revel in him!

Philippians 4:4 MSG

A happy heart is like a continual feast.

Proverbs 15:15 NCV

If they serve Him obediently, they will end their days in prosperity and their years in happiness.

Job 36:11 HCSB

The one who understands a matter finds success, and the one who trusts in the Lord will be happy.

Proverbs 16:20 HCSB

SOME BIG IDEAS

Joy is the great note all throughout the Bible.

Oswald Chambers

Some of us seem so anxious about avoiding hell that we forget to celebrate our journey toward heaven.

Philip Yancey

If you can forgive the person you were, accept the person you are, and believe in the person you will become, you are headed for joy. So celebrate your life.

Barbara Johnson

Unparalleled joy and victory come from allowing Christ to do "the hard thing" with us.

Beth Moore

God has given you the gift of life (here on earth) and the promise of eternal life (in heaven). Now, He wants you to celebrate those gifts. By celebrating the gift of life, you protect your heart from the dangers of pessimism, regret, hopelessness, and bitterness.

GOD DOESN'T CHANGE

For I am the Lord, I do not change.

Malachi 3:6 NKJV

We live in a world that is always changing, but we worship a God who never changes—thank goodness! That means we can be comforted in the knowledge that our Heavenly Father is the rock that simply cannot be moved: "I am the Lord, I do not change" (Malachi 3:6 NKJV).

The next time you face difficult circumstances, tough times, unfair treatment, or unwelcome changes, remember that some things never change—things like the love that you feel in your heart for your family and friends . . . and the love that God feels for you. So, instead of worrying too much about life's inevitable challenges, focus your energies on finding solutions. Have faith in your own abilities, do your best to solve your problems, and leave the rest up to God.

IN
OUT

FOLLOW

MORE FROM GOD'S WORD

The sensible see danger and take cover; the foolish keep going and are punished.

Proverbs 27:12 HCSB

But may the God of all grace, who called us to His eternal glory by Christ Jesus, after you have suffered a while, perfect, establish, strengthen, and settle you.

1 Peter 5:10 NKJV

Therefore we do not lose heart. Even though our outward man is perishing, yet the inward man is being renewed day by day.

2 Corinthians 4:16 NKJV

Create in me a clean heart, O God, and renew a steadfast spirit within me.

Psalm 51:10 NKJV

NEXT

SOME BIG IDEAS

The secret of contentment in the midst of change is found in having roots in the changeless Christ—the same yesterday, today and forever.

Ed Young

The resurrection of Jesus Christ is the power of God to change history and to change lives.

Bill Bright

The world continues to change, as do you. Change is inevitable—you can either roll with it or be rolled over by it. In order to avoid the latter, you should choose the former . . . and trust God as you go.

Conditions are always changing; therefore, I must not be dependent upon conditions. What matters supremely is my soul and my relationship to God.

Corrie ten Boom

With God, it isn't who you were that matters; it's who you are becoming.

Liz Curtis Higgs

WHEN YOU HAVE QUESTIONS, YOU CAN TAKE THEM TO GOD

Now if any of you lacks wisdom, he should ask God, who gives to all generously and without criticizing, and it will be given to him. But let him ask in faith without doubting. For the doubter is like the surging sea, driven and tossed by the wind.

James 1:5-6 HCSB

So many questions and so few answers! If that statement seems to describe the current state of your spiritual life, don't panic. Even the most faithful Christians are overcome by occasional bouts of fear and doubt. You are no different.

When you feel that your faith is being tested to its limits, seek the comfort and assurance of the One who sent His Son as a sacrifice for you. And remember: Even when you feel very distant from God, God is never distant from you. When you sincerely seek His presence, He will touch your heart, calm your fears, and restore your soul.

MORE FROM GOD'S WORD

We are pressured in every way but not crushed; we are perplexed but not in despair.

2 Corinthians 4:8 HCSB

Never be afraid to ask questions—lots of questions. It's better to ask a question (and appear ignorant for five minutes) than not to ask a question (and remain ignorant for a lifetime).

But the wisdom from above is first pure, then peace-loving, gentle, compliant, full of mercy and good fruits, without favoritism and hypocrisy.

James 3:17 HCSB

Lord, I turn my hope to You. My God, I trust in You.

Psalm 25:1-2 HCSB

So those who suffer according to God's will should, in doing good, entrust themselves to a faithful Creator.

1 Peter 4:19 HCSB

ENTER
EXIT

100 ESSENTIAL DEVOS FOR TWEENS

SOME BIG IDEAS

When there is perplexity there is always guidance—
not always at the moment we ask, but in good time,
which is God's time. There is no need to fret and stew.

Elisabeth Elliot

We are finding we don't have such a gnawing need to
know the answers when we know the Answer.

Gloria Gaither

Be to the world a sign that while we as Christians do
not have all the answers, we do know and care about
the questions.

Billy Graham

Be still: pause and discover that God is God.

Charles Swindoll

41

GOD CAN HANDLE IT

Give your burdens to the Lord, and he will take care of you. He will not permit the godly to slip and fall.

Psalm 55:22 NLT

It's a promise that is made over and over again in the Bible: Whatever "it" is, God can handle it.

Life isn't always easy. Far from it! Sometimes, life can be very, very tough. But even then, even during our darkest moments, we're protected by a loving Heavenly Father. When we're worried, God can reassure us; when we're sad, God can comfort us. When our hearts are broken, God is not just near, He is here. So we must lift our thoughts and prayers to Him. When we do, He will answer our prayers. Why? Because He is our Shepherd, and He has promised to protect us now and forever.

MORE FROM GOD'S WORD

We also have joy with our troubles, because we know that these troubles produce patience. And patience produces character, and character produces hope.

Romans 5:3-4 NCV

Don't fret or worry. Instead of worrying, pray. Let petitions and praises shape your worries into prayers, letting God know your concerns. Before you know it, a sense of God's wholeness, everything coming together for good, will come and settle you down. It's wonderful what happens when Christ displaces worry at the center of your life.

Philippians 4:6-7 MSG

The Lord lifts the burdens of those bent beneath their loads. The Lord loves the righteous.

Psalm 146:8 NLT

We are pressured in every way but not crushed; we are perplexed but not in despair.

2 Corinthians 4:8 HCSB

43

SOME BIG IDEAS

You may not know what you are going to do; you only know that God knows what He is going to do.

Oswald Chambers

If you're having tough times, don't hit the panic button and don't keep everything bottled up inside. Find a person you can really trust, and talk things over. A second opinion (or, for that matter, a third, fourth, or fifth opinion) is usually helpful.

The next time you're disappointed, don't panic. Don't give up. Just be patient and let God remind you he's still in control.

Max Lucado

Jesus does not say, "There is no storm." He says, "I am here, do not toss, but trust."

Vance Havner

Your greatest ministry will likely come out of your greatest hurt.

Rick Warren

THE BIBLE IS
A BOOK UNLIKE
ANY OTHER

For I am not ashamed of the gospel, because it is God's power for salvation to everyone who believes.

Romans 1:16 HCSB

The Bible can be a powerful tool for strengthening our faith. George Mueller observed, "The vigor of our spiritual lives will be in exact proportion to the place held by the Bible in our lives and in our thoughts." As Christians, we are called upon to study God's Holy Word and then apply it to our lives. When we do, we are blessed.

The Bible is a priceless gift, a tool for Christians to use as they share the Good News of their Savior, Christ Jesus. Too many Christians, however, keep their spiritual tool kits tightly closed and out of sight. Jonathan Edwards advised, "Be assiduous in reading the Holy Scriptures. This is the fountain whence all knowledge in divinity must be derived. Therefore let not this

treasure lie by you neglected." God's Holy Word is, indeed, a priceless, one-of-a-kind treasure. Handle it with care, but, more importantly, handle it every day.

MORE FROM GOD'S WORD

All Scripture is inspired by God and is profitable for teaching, for rebuking, for correcting, for training in righteousness, so that the man of God may be complete, equipped for every good work.

2 Timothy 3:16-17 HCSB

Man shall not live by bread alone, but by every word that proceeds from the mouth of God.

Matthew 4:4 NKJV

For the word of God is living and effective and sharper than any two-edged sword, penetrating as far as to divide soul, spirit, joints, and marrow; it is a judge of the ideas and thoughts of the heart.

Hebrews 4:12 HCSB

ENTER
EXIT

OPEN THE GOOD BOOK

Do you have any favorite verses from the Bible? Take a few minutes and look them up again and jot them down below. While you're at it, find a few more verses or stories that speak to you.

_____

_____

_____

_____

_____

_____

_____

_____

_____

_____

_____

_____

NEXT

SOME BIG IDEAS

The instrument of our sanctification is the Word of God. The Spirit of God brings to our minds the precepts and doctrines of truth, and applies them with power. The truth is our sanctifier. If we do not hear or read it, we will not grow in sanctification.

C. H. Spurgeon

God gives us a compass and a Book of promises and principles—the Bible—and lets us make our decisions day by day as we sense the leading of His Spirit. This is how we grow.

Warren Wiersbe

The Bible is the one Book to which any thoughtful man may go with any honest question of life or destiny and find the answer of God by honest searching.

John Ruskin

Take a Bible with you wherever you go. You never know when you may need a midday spiritual pick-me-up.

DEVO 14

ASK GOD FOR HELP

And yet the reason you don't have what you want is that you don't ask God for it.

James 4:2 HCSB

Sometimes, amid the stresses and the frustrations of daily life, we forget to slow ourselves down long enough to talk with God. Instead of turning our thoughts and prayers to Him, we rely entirely upon our own resources, with decidedly mixed results. Or, instead of praying for strength, we seek to manufacture it within ourselves, only to find that lasting strength remains elusive.

Are you in need? Ask God to sustain you. And while you're in the mood to ask, don't be afraid to ask for the loving support of your family and friends. When you ask for help, you're likely to receive it. But if you're unwilling to ask, why should you expect to receive it?

So the next time times get tough, remember that help is on the way . . . all you must do is ask.

MORE FROM GOD'S WORD

If you need wisdom—if you want to know what God wants you to do—ask him, and he will gladly tell you. He will not resent your asking.

James 1:5 NLT

From now on, whatever you request along the lines of who I am and what I am doing, I'll do it. That's how the Father will be seen for who he is in the Son. I mean it. Whatever you request in this way, I'll do.

John 14:13-14 MSG

You did not choose me, but I chose you and appointed you to go and bear fruit—fruit that will last. Then the Father will give you whatever you ask in my name.

John 15:16 NIV

Until now you have not asked for anything in my name. Ask and you will receive, so that your joy will be the fullest possible joy.

John 16:24 NCV

SOME BIG IDEAS

When will we realize that we're not troubling God with our questions and concerns? His heart is open to hear us—his touch nearer than our next thought—as if no one in the world existed but us. Our very personal God wants to hear from us personally.

Gigi Graham Tchividjian

God will help us become the people we are meant to be, if only we will ask Him.

Hannah Whitall Smith

When trials come your way—as inevitably they will—do not run away. Run to your God and Father.

Kay Arthur

Often I have made a request of God with earnest pleadings even backed up with Scripture, only to have Him say "No" because He had something better in store.

Ruth Bell Graham

If you want more from life, ask more from God. If you're seeking a worthy goal, ask for God's help—and keep asking—until He answers your prayers. If you sincerely want to guard your words and your steps, ask for God's help many times each day.

THE CHOICES YOU MAKE ARE IMPORTANT

But the wisdom from above is first pure, then peace-loving, gentle, compliant, full of mercy and good fruits, without favoritism and hypocrisy.

James 3:17 HCSB

Your life is a series of choices. From the instant you wake up in the morning until the moment you nod off to sleep at night, you make countless decisions—decisions about the things you do, decisions about the words you speak, and decisions about the way that you choose to direct your thoughts.

As a believer who has been transformed by the love of Jesus, you have every reason to make wise choices. But sometimes, when the stresses of the daily grind threaten to grind you up and spit you out, you may make choices that are displeasing to God. When you do, you'll pay a price because you'll forfeit the happiness and the peace that might otherwise have been yours.

LOOK

IN

OUT

FOLLOW

So, as you pause to consider the kind of Christian you are—and the kind of Christian you want to become—ask yourself whether you're sitting on the fence or standing in the light. The choice is yours . . . and so are the consequences.

MORE FROM GOD'S WORD

I am offering you life or death, blessings or curses. Now, choose life! . . . To choose life is to love the Lord your God, obey him, and stay close to him.

Deuteronomy 30:19-20 NCV

So I strive always to keep my conscience clear before God and man.

Acts 24:16 NIV

The thing you should want most is God's kingdom and doing what God wants. Then all these other things you need will be given to you.

Matthew 6:33 NCV

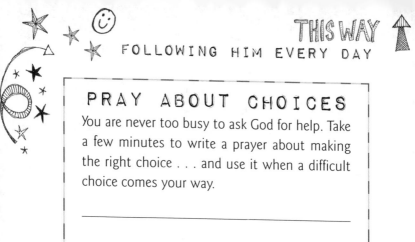

PRAY ABOUT CHOICES

You are never too busy to ask God for help. Take a few minutes to write a prayer about making the right choice . . . and use it when a difficult choice comes your way.

SOME BIG IDEAS

Life is pretty much like a cafeteria line—it offers us many choices, both good and bad. The Christian must have a spiritual radar that detects the difference not only between bad and good but also among good, better, and best.

Dennis Swanberg

The greatest choice any man makes is to let God choose for him.

Vance Havner

Every day, I find countless opportunities to decide whether I will obey God and demonstrate my love for Him or try to please myself or the world system. God is waiting for my choices.

Bill Bright

Little decisions, when taken together over a long period of time, can have big consequences. So remember that when it comes to matters of health, fitness, stress, and spirituality, there are no small decisions.

GOD WANTS YOU TO BE A COURAGEOUS CHRISTIAN

Be strong and courageous, and do the work. Don't be afraid or discouraged, for the Lord God, my God, is with you. He won't leave you or forsake you.

1 Chronicles 28:20 HCSB

Because we are saved by a risen Christ, we can have hope for the future, no matter how desperate our circumstances may seem. After all, God has promised that we are His throughout eternity. And, He has told us that we must place our hopes in Him.

Today, summon the courage to follow God. Even if the path seems difficult, even if your heart is fearful, trust your Heavenly Father and follow Him. Trust Him with your day and your life. Do His work, care for His children, and share His Good News. Let Him guide your steps. He will not lead you astray.

MORE FROM GOD'S WORD

You did not choose Me, but I chose you. I appointed you that you should go out and produce fruit, and that your fruit should remain, so that whatever you ask the Father in My name, He will give you.

John 15:16 HCSB

Then He said to them all, "If anyone wants to come with Me, he must deny himself, take up his cross daily, and follow Me."

Luke 9:23 HCSB

I, therefore, the prisoner in the Lord, urge you to walk worthy of the calling you have received.

Ephesians 4:1 HCSB

Let us lay aside every weight and the sin that so easily ensnares us, and run with endurance the race that lies before us, keeping our eyes on Jesus, the source and perfecter of our faith.

Hebrews 12:1-2 HCSB

SOME BIG IDEAS

Down through the centuries, in times of trouble and trial, God has brought courage to the hearts of those who love Him. The Bible is filled with assurances of God's help and comfort in every kind of trouble which might cause fears to arise in the human heart. You can look ahead with promise, hope, and joy.

Billy Graham

With God as your partner, you have nothing to fear. Why? Because you and God, working together, can handle absolutely anything that comes your way. When you sincerely turn to God, He will never fail you.

Choose Jesus Christ! Deny yourself, take up the Cross, and follow Him—for the world must be shown. The world must see, in us, a discernible, visible, startling difference.

Elisabeth Elliot

Be careful how you live. You may be the only Bible some person ever reads.

William J. Toms

DON'T GET HUNG UP ON APPEARANCES

As the water reflects the face, so the heart reflects the person.

Proverbs 27:19 HCSB

The world sees you as you appear to be; God sees you as you really are. He sees your heart, and He understands your intentions. The opinions of others should be relatively unimportant to you; however, God's view of you—His understanding of your actions, your thoughts, and your motivations—should be vitally important.

Few things in life are more futile than "keeping up appearances" in order to impress your friends and your dates—yet the media would have you believe otherwise. The media would have you believe that everything depends on the color of your hair, the condition of your wardrobe, and the model of the car you drive. But nothing could be further from the truth. What is important, of course, is pleasing your Father in heaven.

You please Him when your intentions are pure and your actions are just. When you do, you will be blessed today, tomorrow, and forever.

MORE FROM GOD'S WORD

And why worry about your clothes? Look at the lilies and how they grow. They don't work or make their clothing, yet Solomon in all his glory was not dressed as beautifully as they are.

Matthew 6:28-29 NLT

The LORD doesn't make decisions the way you do! People judge by outward appearance, but the LORD looks at a person's thoughts and intentions.

1 Samuel 16:7 NLT

We justify our actions by appearances; God examines our motives.

Proverbs 21:2 MSG

As the water reflects the face, so the heart reflects the person.

Proverbs 27:19 HCSB

SOME BIG IDEAS

If the narrative of the Scriptures teaches us anything, from the serpent in the Garden to the carpenter in Nazareth, it teaches us that things are rarely what they seem, that we shouldn't be fooled by appearances.

John Eldredge

Too many Christians have geared their program to please, to entertain, and to gain favor from this world. We are concerned with how much, instead of how little, like this age we can become.

Billy Graham

Fashion is an enduring testimony to the fact that we live quite consciously before the eyes of others.

John Eldredge

When making judgments about friends and other people, don't focus on appearances, focus on values.

61

CHARACTER COUNTS

In all things showing yourself to be a pattern of good works; in doctrine showing integrity, reverence, incorruptibility . . . .

Titus 2:7 NKJV

Beth Moore correctly observed, "Those who walk in truth walk in liberty." Godly guys and girls agree. As believers in Christ, we must seek to live each day with discipline, honesty, and faith. When we do, at least two things happen: integrity becomes a habit, and God blesses us because of our obedience to Him. Living a life of integrity isn't always the easiest way, but in the long run, it's the more peaceful—and less stressful—way to live.

Character isn't built overnight; it is built slowly over a lifetime. It is the sum of every sensible choice, every honorable decision, and every honest word. It is forged on the anvil of sincerity and polished by the virtue of fairness. Character is a precious thing—preserve yours at all costs.

MORE FROM GOD'S WORD

As the water reflects the face, so the heart reflects the person.

Proverbs 27:19 HCSB

We also rejoice in our afflictions, because we know that affliction produces endurance, endurance produces proven character, and proven character produces hope.

Romans 5:3-4 HCSB

A good name is to be chosen rather than great riches, loving favor rather than silver and gold.

Proverbs 22:1 NKJV

Do not be deceived: "Evil company corrupts good habits."

1 Corinthians 15:33 NKJV

> When your words are honest and your intentions are pure, you have nothing to fear. Thus, you should guard your integrity even more carefully than you guard your wallet.

SOME BIG IDEAS

Integrity is the glue that holds our way of life together. We must constantly strive to keep our integrity intact. When wealth is lost, nothing is lost; when health is lost, something is lost; when character is lost, all is lost.

Billy Graham

No man can use his Bible with power unless he has the character of Jesus in his heart.

Alan Redpath

The man who cannot believe in himself cannot believe in anything else. The basis of all integrity and character is whatever faith we have in our own integrity

Roy L. Smith

Image is what people think we are; integrity is what we really are.

John Maxwell

DEVO 19

YOU ARE RICHLY BLESSED

The Lord bless you and keep you; the Lord make His face shine upon you, and be gracious to you.

Numbers 6:24-25 NKJV

Have you counted your blessings lately? If you sincerely wish to follow in Christ's footsteps, you should make thanksgiving a habit, a regular part of your daily routine.

How has God blessed you? First and foremost, He has given you the gift of eternal life through the sacrifice of His only begotten Son, but the blessings don't stop there. Today, take time to make a partial list of the God's gifts to you: the talents, the opportunities, the possessions, and the relationships that you may, on occasion, take for granted. And then, when you've spent sufficient time listing your blessings, offer a prayer of gratitude to the Giver of all things good . . . and, to the best of your ability, use your gifts for the glory of His kingdom.

MORE FROM GOD'S WORD

You will show me the path of life; in Your presence is fullness of joy; at Your right hand are pleasures forevermore.

Psalm 16:11 NKJV

I pray also that you will have greater understanding in your heart so you will know the hope to which he has called us and that you will know how rich and glorious are the blessings God has promised his holy people. And you will know that God's power is very great for us who believe.

Ephesians 1:18-19 NCV

I will bless them and the places surrounding my hill. I will send down showers in season; there will be showers of blessings.

Ezekiel 34:26 NIV

The Lord is kind and merciful, slow to get angry, full of unfailing love. The Lord is good to everyone. He showers compassion on all his creation.

Psalm 145:8-9 NLT

SOME BIG IDEAS

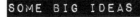

It is when we give ourselves to be a blessing that we can specially count on the blessing of God.

Andrew Murray

We prevent God from giving us the great spiritual gifts He has in store for us, because we do not give thanks for daily gifts.

Dietrich Bonhoeffer

Nobody ever outgrows Scripture; the book widens and deepens with our years.

C. H. Spurgeon

Get rich quick! Count your blessings!

Anonymous

If you need a little cheering up, start counting your blessings. In truth, you really have too many blessings to count, but it never hurts to try.

IT'S IMPORTANT TO BE COURTEOUS

Be hospitable to one another without grumbling.

1 Peter 4:9 NKJV

D id Christ instruct us in matters of etiquette and courtesy? Of course He did. Christ's instructions are clear: "In everything, therefore, treat people the same way you want them to treat you, for this is the Law and the Prophets" (Matthew 7:12 NASB). Jesus did not say, "In some things, treat people as you wish to be treated." And, He did not say, "From time to time, treat others with kindness." Christ said that we should treat others as we wish to be treated in every aspect of our daily lives. This, of course, is a tall order indeed, but as Christians, we are commanded to do our best.

Today, be a little kinder than necessary to family members, friends, and total strangers. And, as you consider all the things that Christ has done in your life, honor Him with your words and with your deeds. He expects no less, and He deserves no less.

MORE FROM GOD'S WORD

Don't criticize one another, brothers. He who criticizes a brother or judges his brother criticizes the law and judges the law. But if you judge the law, you are not a doer of the law but a judge.

James 4:11 HCSB

Are there those among you who are truly wise and understanding? Then they should show it by living right and doing good things with a gentleness that comes from wisdom.

James 3:13 NCV

A good person produces good deeds from a good heart, and an evil person produces evil deeds from an evil heart. Whatever is in your heart determines what you say.

Luke 6:45 NLT

Dear friend, when you extend hospitality to Christian brothers and sisters, even when they are strangers, you make the faith visible.

3 John 1:5 MSG

SOME BIG IDEAS

When you extend hospitality to others, you're not trying to impress people; you're trying to reflect God to them.

Max Lucado

Only the courteous can love, but it is love that makes them courteous.

C. S. Lewis

Remember: courtesy isn't optional. If you disagree, do so without being disagreeable; if you're angry, hold your tongue; if you're frustrated or tired, don't argue . . . take a nap.

Courtesy is contagious.

Marie T. Freeman

If you are willing to honor a person out of respect for God, you can be assured that God will honor you.

Beth Moore

WHEN YOU CAST YOUR BURDENS ON THE LORD, YOU'LL BE VICTORIOUS

Cast your burden upon the Lord and He will sustain you:
He will never allow the righteous to be shaken.

Psalm 55:22 NASB

Your decision to seek a deeper relationship with God will not remove all problems from your life; to the contrary, it will bring about a series of personal crises as you constantly seek to say "yes" to God although the world encourages you to do otherwise. You live in a world that seeks to snare your attention and lead you away from God. Each time you are tempted to distance yourself from the Creator, you will face a spiritual crisis. A few of these crises may be monumental in scope, but most will be the small, everyday decisions of life. In fact, life here on earth can be seen as one test after another—and with each crisis comes

yet another opportunity to grow closer to God . . . or to distance yourself from His plan for your life.

Today, you will face many opportunities to say "yes" to your Creator—and you will also encounter many opportunities to say "no" to Him. Your answers will determine the quality of your day and the direction of your life, so answer carefully . . . very carefully.

MORE FROM GOD'S WORD

We also have joy with our troubles, because we know that these troubles produce patience. And patience produces character, and character produces hope.

Romans 5:3-4 NCV

The LORD also will be a stronghold for the oppressed, a stronghold in times of trouble.

Psalm 9:9 NASB

You pulled me from the brink of death, my feet from the cliff-edge of doom. Now I stroll at leisure with God in the sunlit fields of life.

Psalm 56:13 MSG

SOME BIG IDEAS

We all go through pain and sorrow, but the presence of God, like a warm, comforting blanket, can shield us and protect us, and allow the deep inner joy to surface, even in the most devastating circumstances.

Barbara Johnson

Our heavenly Father never takes anything from his children unless he means to give them something better.

George Mueller

> If you're facing a crisis, don't face it alone. Enlist God's help. When you have finished praying about your problem, don't be afraid to seek help from family, from friends, or from your pastor.

Recently I've been learning that life comes down to this: God is in everything. Regardless of what difficulties I am experiencing at the moment, or what things aren't as would like them to be, I look at the circumstances and say, "Lord, what are you trying to teach me?"

Catherine Marshall

IT PAYS TO BE DISCIPLINED

But I discipline my body and bring it into subjection, lest, when I have preached to others, I myself should become disqualified.

1 Corinthians 9:27 NKJV

God doesn't reward laziness, misbehavior, or apathy. To the contrary, He expects His followers to behave with dignity and discipline. But sometimes, it's extremely difficult to be dignified and disciplined. Why? Because the world wants us to believe that dignified, self-disciplined behavior is going out of style.

Face facts: Life's greatest rewards aren't likely to fall into your lap. To the contrary, your greatest accomplishments will probably require lots of work, which is perfectly fine with God. After all, He knows that you're up to the task, and He has big plans for you. God will do His part to fulfill those plans, and the rest, of course, is up to you.

Now, are you steadfast in your determination to be a self-disciplined person? If so, congratulations . . . if not, reread this little essay—and keep reading it—until God's message finally sinks in.

MORE FROM GOD'S WORD

No discipline seems enjoyable at the time, but painful. Later on, however, it yields the fruit of peace and righteousness to those who have been trained by it.

Hebrews 12:11 HCSB

The one who follows instruction is on the path to life, but the one who rejects correction goes astray.

Proverbs 10:17 HCSB

For this very reason, make every effort to supplement your faith with goodness, goodness with knowledge, knowledge with self-control, self-control with endurance, endurance with godliness.

2 Peter 1:5-6 HCSB

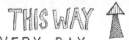

SOME BIG IDEAS

The alternative to discipline is disaster.

Vance Havner

Personal humility is a spiritual discipline and the hallmark of the service of Jesus.

Franklin Graham

> A disciplined lifestyle gives you more control: The more disciplined you become, the more you can take control over your life (which is far better than letting your life take control over you).

Discipline is training that develops and corrects.

Charles Stanley

As we seek to become disciples of Jesus Christ, we should never forget that the word disciple is directly related to the word discipline. To be a disciple of the Lord Jesus Christ is to know his discipline.

Dennis Swanberg

WHEN YOU HAVE DOUBTS, TAKE THEM TO GOD

Though I sit in darkness, the Lord will be my light.

Micah 7:8 HCSB

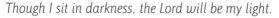

Doubts come in several shapes and sizes: doubts about God, doubts about the future, and doubts about our own abilities, for starters. But when doubts creep in, as they will from time to time, we need not despair. As Sheila Walsh observed, "To wrestle with God does not mean that we have lost faith, but that we are fighting for it."

God never leaves our side, not for an instant. He is always with us, always willing to calm the storms of life. When we sincerely seek His presence—and when we genuinely seek to establish a deeper, more meaningful relationship with Him—God is prepared to touch our hearts, to calm our fears, to answer our doubts, and to restore our confidence.

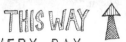
MORE FROM GOD'S WORD

If you don't know what you're doing, pray to the Father. He loves to help. You'll get his help, and won't be condescended to when you ask for it. Ask boldly, believingly, without a second thought. People who "worry their prayers" are like wind-whipped waves. Don't think you're going to get anything from the Master that way, adrift at sea, keeping all your options open.

James 1:5-8 MSG

Immediately the father of the boy cried out, "I do believe! Help my unbelief."

Mark 9:24 HCSB

Come! He said. And climbing out of the boat, Peter started walking on the water and came toward Jesus. But when he saw the strength of the wind, he was afraid. And beginning to sink he cried out, "Lord, save me!" Immediately Jesus reached out His hand, caught hold of him, and said to him, "You of little faith, why did you doubt?" When they got into the boat, the wind ceased.

Matthew 14:29-32 HCSB

SOME BIG IDEAS

Mark it down. God never turns away the honest seeker. Go to God with your questions. You may not find all the answers, but in finding God, you know the One who does.

Max Lucado

Doubting may temporarily disturb, but will not permanently destroy, your faith in Christ.

Charles Swindoll

Feelings of uselessness and hopelessness are not from God, but from the evil one, the devil, who wants to discourage you and thwart your effectiveness for the Lord.

Bill Bright

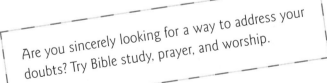

Are you sincerely looking for a way to address your doubts? Try Bible study, prayer, and worship.

TODAY IS A NEW BEGINNING

You are being renewed in the spirit of your minds; you put on the new man, the one created according to God's likeness in righteousness and purity of the truth.

Ephesians 4:23-24 HCSB

Each new day offers countless opportunities to serve God, to seek His will, and to obey His teachings. But each day also offers countless opportunities to stray from God's commandments and to wander far from His path.

Sometimes, we wander aimlessly in a wilderness of our own making, but God has better plans for us. And, whenever we ask Him to renew our strength and guide our steps, He does so.

Consider this day a new beginning. Consider it a fresh start, a renewed opportunity to serve your Creator with willing hands and a loving heart. Ask God to renew your sense of purpose as He guides your steps. Today is a glorious opportunity to serve God. Seize that opportunity while you can.

MORE FROM GOD'S WORD

Then the One seated on the throne said, "Look! I am making everything new."

Revelation 21:5 HCSB

But those who wait on the Lord shall renew their strength; they shall mount up with wings like eagles, they shall run and not be weary, they shall walk and not faint.

Isaiah 40:31 NKJV

Therefore if anyone is in Christ, he is a new creature; the old things passed away; behold, new things have come.

2 Corinthians 5:17 HCSB

Therefore, this is what the Lord says: If you return, I will restore you; you will stand in My presence.

Jeremiah 15:19 HCSB

SOME BIG IDEAS

No matter how badly we have failed, we can always get up and begin again. Our God is the God of new beginnings.

Warren Wiersbe

Sometimes your medicine bottle has on it, "Shake well before using." That is what God has to do with some of His people. He has to shake them well before they are ever usable.

Vance Havner

More often than not, when something looks like it's the absolute end, it is really the beginning.

Charles Swindoll

God wants to give you peace, and He wants to renew your spirit. It's up to you to slow down and give Him a chance to do so.

STAND UP FOR YOUR BELIEFS

I know whom I have believed and am persuaded that He is able to guard what has been entrusted to me until that day.

2 Timothy 1:12 HCSB

In describing one's beliefs, actions are far better descriptors than words. Yet far too many of us spend more energy talking about our beliefs than living by them—with predictable consequences.

Is your life a picture book of your creed? Are your actions congruent with your beliefs? Are you willing to practice the philosophy that you preach? If so, you'll most certainly feel better about yourself.

Today and every day, make certain that your actions are guided by God's Word and by the conscience that He has placed in your heart. Don't treat your faith as if it were separate from your everyday life. Weave your beliefs into the very fabric of your day. When you do, God will honor your good works, and your good works will honor God.

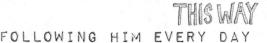
MORE FROM GOD'S WORD

Everyone who believes that Jesus is the Messiah has been born of God, and everyone who loves the parent also loves his child.

1 John 5:1 HCSB

Then Jesus told the centurion, "Go. As you have believed, let it be done for you." And his servant was cured that very moment.

Matthew 8:13 HCSB

All things are possible to him that believeth.

Mark 9:23 KJV

You never saw him, yet you love him. You still don't see him, yet you trust him—with laughter and singing. Because you kept on believing, you'll get what you're looking forward to: total salvation.

1 Peter 1:8-9 MSG

SOME BIG IDEAS

God's presence is with you, but you have to make a choice to believe—and I mean, really believe—that this is true. This conscious decision is yours alone.

Bill Hybels

Belief is not the result of an intellectual act; it is the result of an act of my will whereby I deliberately commit myself.

Oswald Chambers

You may as well quit reading and hearing the Word of God and give it to the devil if you do not desire to live according to it.

Martin Luther

When you stand up for your beliefs—and when you follow your conscience—you'll feel better about yourself. When you don't, you won't.

I do not seek to understand that I may believe, but I believe in order to understand.

St. Augustine

FULLY GROWN?

So let us stop going over the basics of Christianity again and again. Let us go on instead and become mature in our understanding.

Hebrews 6:1 NLT

Are you about as mature as you're ever going to be? Hopefully not! When it comes to your faith, God doesn't intend for you to become "fully grown," at least not in this lifetime.

As a Christian, you should continue to grow in the love and the knowledge of your Savior as long as you live. How? By studying God's Word, by obeying His commandments, and by allowing His Son to reign over your heart.

Are you continually seeking to become a more mature believer? Hopefully so, because that's exactly what you owe to God and to yourself.

MORE FROM GOD'S WORD

For this reason also, since the day we heard this, we haven't stopped praying for you. We are asking that you may be filled with the knowledge of His will in all wisdom and spiritual understanding.

Colossians 1:9 HCSB

But grow in the grace and knowledge of our Lord and Savior Jesus Christ. To Him be the glory both now and to the day of eternity.

2 Peter 3:18 HCSB

I want their hearts to be encouraged and joined together in love, so that they may have all the riches of assured understanding, and have the knowledge of God's mystery—Christ.

Colossians 2:2 HCSB

Now may the God of hope fill you with all joy and peace in believing, so that you may overflow with hope by the power of the Holy Spirit.

Romans 15:13 HCSB

NEXT

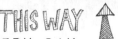
SOME BIG IDEAS

A person who gazes and keeps on gazing at Jesus becomes like him in appearance.

E. Stanley Jones

The Scriptures were not given for our information, but for our transformation.

D. L. Moody

> If you're determined to keep growing spiritually, you'll feel better about your world, your faith, and yourself. So keep growing . . . or else.

Approach the Scriptures not so much as a manual of Christian principles but as the testimony of God's friends on what it means to walk with him through a thousand different episodes.

John Eldredge

Be filled with the Holy Spirit; join a church where the members believe the Bible and know the Lord; seek the fellowship of other Christians; learn and be nourished by God's Word and His many promises. Conversion is not the end of your journey—it is only the beginning.

Corrie ten Boom

NOTHING CAN SEPARATE US FROM CHRIST'S LOVE

For I am persuaded that neither death nor life, nor angels nor rulers, nor things present, nor things to come, nor powers, nor height, nor depth, nor any other created thing will have the power to separate us from the love of God that is in Christ Jesus our Lord!

Romans 8:38-39 HCSB

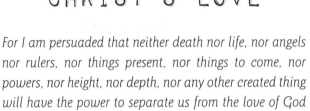

ow much does Christ love us? More than we, as mere mortals, can comprehend. His love is perfect and steadfast. Even though we are imperfect and wayward, the Good Shepherd cares for us still. Even though we have fallen far short of the Father's commandments, Christ loves us with a power and depth that are beyond our understanding. The sacrifice that Jesus made upon the cross was made for each of us, and His love endures for eternity and beyond.

Christ's love changes everything, including your relationships. When you accept His gift of grace, you

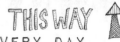
are transformed, not only for today, but also for all eternity.

Jesus is waiting patiently for you to invite Him into your heart. Please don't make Him wait a single minute longer.

MORE FROM GOD'S WORD

I am the good shepherd. The good shepherd lays down his life for the sheep.

John 10:11 HCSB

Then he told them what they could expect for themselves: "Anyone who intends to come with me has to let me lead."

Luke 9:23 MSG

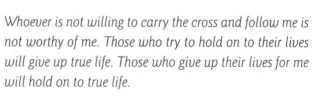

Whoever is not willing to carry the cross and follow me is not worthy of me. Those who try to hold on to their lives will give up true life. Those who give up their lives for me will hold on to true life.

Matthew 10:38-39 NCV

SOME BIG IDEAS

He loved us not because we're lovable, but because He is love.

C. S. Lewis

God expressed His love in sending the Holy Spirit to live within us.

Charles Stanley

God is my heavenly Father. He loves me with an everlasting love. The proof of that is the Cross.

Elisabeth Elliot

Live your lives in love, the same sort of love which Christ gives us, and which He perfectly expressed when He gave Himself as a sacrifice to God.

Corrie ten Boom

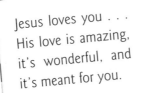

Jesus loves you . . .
His love is amazing,
it's wonderful, and
it's meant for you.

IT PAYS TO GET INVOLVED AT CHURCH

And I also say to you that you are Peter, and on this rock I will build My church, and the forces of Hades will not overpower it. I will give you the keys of the kingdom of heaven, and whatever you bind on earth will have been bound in heaven, and whatever you loose on earth will have been loosed in heaven.

Matthew 16:18-19 HCSB

A good way to figure out the kind of person you want to become is by worshiping with people who love and respect you. That's one reason (but certainly not the only reason) that you should be an active member of a supportive congregation.

Every believer—including you—needs to be part of a community of faith. Your association with fellow Christians should be uplifting, enlightening, encouraging, and consistent.

Are you an active member of your fellowship? Are you a builder of bridges inside the four walls of your

church and outside it? Do you contribute your time and your talents to a close-knit band of hope-filled believers? Hopefully so. The fellowship of believers is intended to be a powerful tool for spreading God's Good News and uplifting His children. God intends for you to be a fully contributing member of that fellowship. Your intentions should be the same.

MORE FROM GOD'S WORD

For we are God's fellow workers; you are God's field, you are God's building.

1 Corinthians 3:9 NKJV

Be on guard for yourselves and for all the flock, among whom the Holy Spirit has appointed you as overseers, to shepherd the church of God, which He purchased with His own blood.

Acts 20:28 HCSB

I rejoiced with those who said to me, "Let us go to the house of the Lord."

Psalm 122:1 HCSB

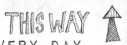

SOME BIG IDEAS

The church has no greater need today than to fall in love with Jesus all over again.

Vance Havner

Only participation in the full life of a local church builds spiritual muscle.

Rick Warren

If you become a fully participating member of an active congregation, you'll become more excited about your faith, your world, and yourself. So do yourself a favor: be an active member of your fellowship.

In God's economy you will be hard-pressed to find many examples of successful "Lone Rangers."

Luci Swindoll

The Bible knows nothing of solitary religion.

John Wesley

DEVO 29

LISTEN CAREFULLY TO YOUR CONSCIENCE

Now the goal of our instruction is love from a pure heart, a good conscience, and a sincere faith.

1 Timothy 1:5 HCSB

B illy Graham correctly observed, "Most of us follow our conscience as we follow a wheelbarrow. We push it in front of us in the direction we want to go." To do so, of course, is a profound mistake. Yet all of us, on occasion, have failed to listen to the voice that God planted in our hearts, and all of us have suffered the consequences.

God gave you a conscience for a very good reason: to make your path conform to His will. Wise believers make it a practice to listen carefully to that quiet internal voice. Count yourself among that number. When your conscience speaks, listen and learn. In all likelihood, God is trying to get His message through. And in all likelihood, it is a message that you desperately need to hear.

ENTER
EXIT

FOLLOW

MORE FROM GOD'S WORD

I always do my best to have a clear conscience toward God and men.

Acts 24:16 HCSB

Let us draw near with a true heart in full assurance of faith, our hearts sprinkled clean from an evil conscience and our bodies washed in pure water.

Hebrews 10:22 HCSB

I will cling to my righteousness and never let it go. My conscience will not accuse [me] as long as I live!

Job 27:6 HCSB

Behold, the kingdom of God is within you.

Luke 17:21 KJV

SOME BIG IDEAS

To go against one's conscience is neither safe nor right. Here I stand. I cannot do otherwise.

Martin Luther

The convicting work of the Holy Spirit awakens, disturbs, and judges.

Franklin Graham

A good conscience is a continual feast.

Francis Bacon

God desires that we become spiritually healthy enough through faith to have a conscience that rightly interprets the work of the Holy Spirit.

Beth Moore

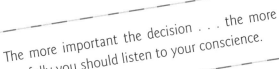

The more important the decision . . . the more carefully you should listen to your conscience.

FINDING
FULFILLMENT

I am the Gate. Anyone who goes through me will be cared for—will freely go in and out, and find pasture. A thief is only there to steal and kill and destroy. I came so they can have real and eternal life, more and better life than they ever dreamed of. "I am the Good Shepherd. The Good Shepherd puts the sheep before himself, sacrifices himself if necessary."

John 10:9-11 MSG

Where can we find fulfillment and contentment? Is it a result of wealth, or power, or beauty, or fame? Hardly. Genuine contentment is a gift from God to those who trust Him and follow His commandments.

Our modern world seems preoccupied with the search for happiness. We are bombarded with messages telling us that happiness depends upon the acquisition of material possessions. These messages are false. Enduring peace is not the result of our acquisitions; it is a spiritual gift from God to those who obey Him and accept His will.

If we don't find contentment in God, we will never find it anywhere else. But, if we seek Him and obey Him, we will be blessed with an inner peace that is beyond human understanding. When God dwells at the center of our lives, peace and contentment will belong to us just as surely as we belong to God.

MORE FROM GOD'S WORD

I have learned to be content in whatever circumstances I am.

Philippians 4:11 HCSB

A tranquil heart is life to the body, but jealousy is rottenness to the bones.

Proverbs 14:30 HCSB

The LORD will give strength to His people; the LORD will bless His people with peace.

Psalm 29:11 NKJV

NEXT

SOME BIG IDEAS

God is most glorified in us when we are most satisfied in him.

John Piper

We are never more fulfilled than when our longing for God is met by His presence in our lives.

Billy Graham

We will never be happy until we make God the source of our fulfillment and the answer to our longings.

Stormie Omartian

By trying to grab fulfillment everywhere, we find it nowhere.

Elisabeth Elliot

If you're not content, try focusing less on "stuff" and more on God.

100

DEVO 31

PRAISE HIM!

I will praise You with my whole heart.

Psalm 138:1 NKJV

If you're like most folks on the planet, you're busy. Your life is probably hectic, demanding, and complicated. And when the demands of life leave you rushing from place to place with scarcely a moment to spare, you may not take time to praise your Creator. Big mistake.

The Bible makes it clear: it pays to praise God. Worship and praise should be a part of everything you do. Otherwise, you quickly lose perspective as you fall prey to the demands of everyday life.

Do you sincerely desire to know God in a more meaningful way? Then praise Him for who He is and for what He has done for you. And please don't wait until Sunday morning—praise Him all day long, every day, for as long as you live . . . and then for all eternity.

ENTER
EXIT

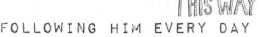
MORE FROM GOD'S WORD

Praise the Lord! Oh, give thanks to the Lord, for He is good! For His mercy endures forever.

Psalm 106:1 NKJV

From the rising of the sun to its going down the Lord's name is to be praised.

Psalm 113:3 NKJV

Enter into His gates with thanksgiving, and into His courts with praise. Be thankful to Him, and bless His name. For the Lord is good; His mercy is everlasting, and His truth endures to all generations.

Psalm 100:4-5 NKJV

So that at the name of Jesus every knee should bow— of those who are in heaven and on earth and under the earth—and every tongue should confess that Jesus Christ is Lord, to the glory of God the Father.

Philippians 2:10-11 HCSB

OUT

SOME BIG IDEAS

Two wings are necessary to lift our souls toward God: prayer and praise. Prayer asks. Praise accepts the answer.

Mrs. Charles E. Cowman

Praise opens the window of our hearts, preparing us to walk more closely with God. Prayer raises the window of our spirit, enabling us to listen more clearly to the Father.

Max Lucado

Most of the verses written about praise in God's Word were voiced by people faced with crushing heartaches, injustice, treachery, slander, and scores of other difficult situations.

Joni Eareckson Tada

> All of your talents and opportunities come from God. Give Him thanks, and give Him the Glory.

When there is peace in the heart, there will be praise on the lips.

Warren Wiersbe

EVIL EXISTS AND IT'S DANGEROUS

Take your stand with God's loyal community and live, or chase after phantoms of evil and die.

Proverbs 11:19 MSG

The better you get to know God, the more you'll understand how God wants you to respond to evil. And make no mistake, this world is inhabited by quite a few people who are very determined to do evil things. The devil and his human helpers are working 24/7 to cause pain and heartbreak in every corner of the globe . . . including your corner. So you'd better beware.

Your job, if you choose to accept it, is to recognize evil and fight it. The moment that you decide to fight evil whenever you see it, you can no longer be a lukewarm, halfhearted Christian. And, when you are no longer a lukewarm Christian, God rejoices while the devil despairs.

When will you choose to get serious about fighting the evils of our world? Before you answer that question, consider this: in the battle of good versus evil, the devil never takes a day off . . . and neither should you.

MORE FROM GOD'S WORD

Be sober! Be on the alert! Your adversary the Devil is prowling around like a roaring lion, looking for anyone he can devour.

1 Peter 5:8 HCSB

Therefore, submit to God. But resist the Devil, and he will flee from you. Draw near to God, and He will draw near to you. Cleanse your hands, sinners, and purify your hearts, double-minded people!

James 4:7-8 HCSB

This High Priest of ours understands our weaknesses, for he faced all of the same temptations we do, yet he did not sin.

Hebrews 4:15 NLT

NEXT

105

SOME BIG IDEAS

Rebuke the Enemy in your own name and he laughs; command him in the name of Christ and he flees.

John Eldredge

Of two evils, choose neither.

C. H. Spurgeon

Evil does exist, and you will confront it. Prepare yourself by forming a genuine, life-changing relationship with God and His only begotten Son. There is darkness in this world, but God's light can overpower any darkness.

He who passively accepts evil is as much involved in it as he who helps to perpetrate it. He who accepts evil without protesting against it is really cooperating with it.

Martin Luther King, Jr.

God loves you, and He yearns for you to turn away from the path of evil. You need His forgiveness, and you need Him to come into your life and remake you from within.

Billy Graham

BE A HUMBLE DISCIPLE

He has told you men what is good and what it is the Lord requires of you: Only to act justly, to love faithfulness, and to walk humbly with your God.

Micah 6:8 HCSB

When Jesus addressed His disciples, He warned that each one must, "take up his cross and follow me." The disciples must have known exactly what the Master meant. In Jesus' day, prisoners were forced to carry their own crosses to the location where they would be put to death. Thus, Christ's message was clear: in order to follow Him, Christ's disciples must deny themselves and, instead, trust Him completely. Nothing has changed since then.

If we are to be disciples of Christ, we must trust Him and place Him at the very center of our beings. Jesus never comes "next." He is always first.

Do you seek to be a worthy disciple of Christ? Then pick up His cross today and every day that you live. When you do, He will bless you now and forever.

MORE FROM GOD'S WORD

Be imitators of God, therefore, as dearly loved children.

Ephesians 5:1 NIV

Work hard, but not just to please your masters when they are watching. As slaves of Christ, do the will of God with all your heart. Work with enthusiasm, as though you were working for the Lord rather than for people.

Ephesians 6:6-7 NLT

Then Jesus said to His disciples, "If anyone wants to come with Me, he must deny himself, take up his cross, and follow Me."

Matthew 16:24 HCSB

All of us who look forward to his Coming stay ready, with the glistening purity of Jesus' life as a model for our own.

1 John 3:3 MSG

SOME BIG IDEAS

Discipleship is a daily discipline: we follow Jesus a step at a time, a day at a time.

Warren Wiersbe

Discipleship means personal, passionate devotion to a Person, our Lord Jesus Christ.

Oswald Chambers

Discipleship is a decision to live by what I know about God, not by what I feel about him or myself or my neighbors.

Eugene Peterson

> Jesus has invited you to become His disciple. If you accept His invitation—and if you obey His commandments—you will be protected and blessed.

Discipleship means allegiance to the suffering Christ, and it is therefore not at all surprising that Christians should be called upon to suffer.

Dietrich Bonhoeffer

IT PAYS TO CONTROL YOUR TEMPER

My dear brothers and sisters, be quick to listen, slow to speak, and slow to get angry. Your anger can never make things right in God's sight.

James 1:19-20 NLT

Temper tantrums are usually unproductive, unattractive, unforgettable, and unnecessary. Perhaps that's why Proverbs 16:32 states that, "Controlling your temper is better than capturing a city" (NCV).

If you've allowed anger to become a regular visitor at your house, you should pray for wisdom, for patience, and for a heart that is so filled with forgiveness that it contains no room for bitterness. God will help you terminate your tantrums if you ask Him to—and that's a good thing because anger and peace cannot coexist in the same mind.

If you permit yourself to throw too many tantrums, you will forfeit—at least for now—the peace that might otherwise be yours through Christ. So obey

God's Word by turning away from anger today and every day. You'll be glad you did, and so will your family and friends.

MORE FROM GOD'S WORD

Don't become angry quickly, because getting angry is foolish.

Ecclesiastes 7:9 NCV

When you are angry, do not sin, and be sure to stop being angry before the end of the day. Do not give the devil a way to defeat you.

Ephesians 4:26–27 NCV

God's servant must not be argumentative, but a gentle listener and a teacher who keeps cool, working firmly but patiently with those who refuse to obey. You never know how or when God might sober them up with a change of heart and a turning to the truth.

2 Timothy 2:24-25 MSG

A patient person [shows] great understanding, but a quick-tempered one promotes foolishness.

Proverbs 14:29 HCSB

111

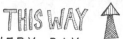
SOME BIG IDEAS

Life is too short to spend it being angry, bored, or dull.

Barbara Johnson

If you're angry with someone, don't say the first thing that comes to your mind. Instead, catch your breath and start counting until you are once again in control of your temper. If you count to a thousand and you're still counting, go to bed! You'll feel better in the morning.

Anger unresolved will only bring you woe.

Kay Arthur

Anger is the noise of the soul; the unseen irritant of the heart; the relentless invader of silence.

Max Lucado

When you strike out in anger, you may miss the other person, but you will always hit yourself.

Jim Gallery

IT PAYS TO BE COURAGEOUS

I sought the Lord, and He answered me and delivered me from all my fears.

Psalm 34:4 HCSB

We live in a world that is, at times, a frightening place. We live in a world that is, at times, a discouraging place. We live in a world where life-changing losses can be so painful and so profound that it seems we will never recover. But, with God's help, and with the help of encouraging family members and friends, we can recover.

During the darker days of life, we are wise to remember the words of Jesus, who reassured His disciples, saying, "Take courage! It is I. Don't be afraid" (Matthew 14:27 NIV). Then, with God's comfort and His love in our hearts, we can offer encouragement to others. And by helping them face their fears, we can, in turn, tackle our own problems with courage, determination, and faith.

MORE FROM GOD'S WORD

Don't be afraid, because I am your God. I will make you strong and will help you; I will support you with my right hand that saves you.

Isaiah 41:10 NCV

Don't be afraid, because the Lord your God will be with you everywhere you go.

Joshua 1:9 NCV

Be strong and courageous, and do the work. Do not be afraid or discouraged, for the Lord God, my God, is with you.

1 Chronicles 28:20 NIV

The Lord is my light and my salvation; whom shall I fear? The Lord is the strength of my life; of whom shall I be afraid?

Psalm 27:1 KJV

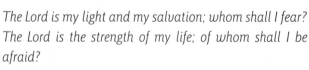

SOME BIG IDEAS

The Lord Jesus by His Holy Spirit is with me, and the knowledge of His presence dispels the darkness and allays any fears.

Bill Bright

When we meditate on God and remember the promises He has given us in His Word, our faith grows, and our fears dissolve.

Charles Stanley

When once we are assured that God is good, then there can be nothing left to fear.

Hannah Whitall Smith

With each new experience of letting God be in control, we gain courage and reinforcement for daring to do it again and again.

Gloria Gaither

> Remember this: a great way to overcome fear is by taking your fears to God . . . and leaving them there.

AIM HIGH

I can do everything through him that gives me strength.
Philippians 4:13 NIV

It takes courage to dream big dreams. You will discover that courage when you do three things: accept the past, trust God to handle the future, and make the most of the time He has given you today.

Are you excited about the opportunities of today and thrilled by the possibilities of tomorrow? Do you confidently expect God to lead you to a place of abundance, peace, and joy? And, when your days on earth are over, do you expect to receive the priceless gift of eternal life? If you trust God's promises, and if you have welcomed God's Son into your heart, then you should believe that your future is intensely and eternally bright.

No dreams are too big for God—not even yours. So start living—and dreaming—accordingly.

MORE FROM GOD'S WORD

Now may the God of hope fill you with all joy and peace in believing, so that you may overflow with hope by the power of the Holy Spirit.

Romans 15:13 HCSB

Where there is no vision, the people perish . . . .

Proverbs 29:18 KJV

Be of good courage, and he shall strengthen your heart, all ye that hope in the LORD.

Psalm 31:24 KJV

Therefore, as we have opportunity, we must work for the good of all, especially for those who belong to the household of faith.

Galatians 6:10 HCSB

NEXT

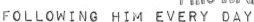
SOME BIG IDEAS

You cannot out-dream God.

John Eldredge

Always stay connected to people and seek out things that bring you joy. Dream with abandon. Pray confidently.

Barbara Johnson

Set goals so big that unless God helps you, you will be a miserable failure.

Bill Bright

The future lies all before us. Shall it only be a slight advance upon what we usually do? Ought it not to be a bound, a leap forward to altitudes of endeavor and success undreamed of before?

Annie Armstrong

Making your dreams come true requires work. John Maxwell writes, "The gap between your vision and your present reality can only be filled through a commitment to maximize your potential." Enough said.

GOD WANTS YOU TO BE GENEROUS

Freely you have received, freely give.

Matthew 10:8 NIV

God's gifts are beyond description, His blessings beyond comprehension. God has been incredibly generous with us, and He rightfully expects us to be generous with others. That's why the thread of generosity is woven into the very fabric of God's teachings.

In the Old Testament, we are told that, "The good person is generous and lends lavishly . . . " (Psalm 112:5 MSG). And in the New Testament we are instructed, "Freely you have received, freely give" (Matthew 10:8 NKJV). These principles still apply. As we establish priorities for our days and our lives, we are advised to give freely of our time, our possessions, and our love—just as God has given freely to us.

Of course, we can never fully repay God for His gifts, but we can share them with others. And we should.

MORE FROM GOD'S WORD

God has given gifts to each of you from his great variety of spiritual gifts. Manage them well so that God's generosity can flow through you.

1 Peter 4:10 NLT

Now this I say, he who sows sparingly will also reap sparingly, and he who sows bountifully will also reap bountifully. Each one must do just as he has purposed in his heart, not grudgingly or under compulsion, for God loves a cheerful giver.

2 Corinthians 9:6-7 NASB

Be generous: Invest in acts of charity. Charity yields high returns.

Ecclesiastes 11:1 MSG

A generous person will be enriched.

Proverbs 11:25 HCSB

SOME BIG IDEAS

The measure of a life, after all, is not its duration but its donation.

Corrie ten Boom

Nothing is really ours until we share it.

C. S. Lewis

A happy spirit takes the grind out of giving. The grease of gusto frees the gears of generosity.

Charles Swindoll

The mind grows by taking in, but the heart grows by giving out.

Warren Wiersbe

> Would you like to be a little happier? Try sharing a few more of the blessings that God has bestowed upon you. In other words, if you want to be happy, be generous. And if you want to be unhappy, be greedy.

THE POWER OF ENCOURAGEMENT

Pleasant words are like a honeycomb, Sweetness to the soul and health to the bones.

Proverbs 16:24 NKJV

Life is a team sport, and all of us need occasional pats on the back from our teammates. As Christians, we are called upon to spread the Good News of Christ, and we are also called to spread a message of encouragement and hope to the world.

Whether you realize it or not, many people with whom you come in contact every day are in desperate need of a smile or an encouraging word. The world can be a difficult place, and countless friends and family members may be troubled by the challenges of everyday life. Since you don't always know who needs your help, the best strategy is to try to encourage all the people who cross your path. So today, be a world-class source of encouragement to everyone you meet. Never has the need been greater.

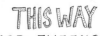

MORE FROM GOD'S WORD

But encourage each other daily, while it is still called today, so that none of you is hardened by sin's deception.

Hebrews 3:13 HCSB

Therefore encourage one another and build each other up as you are already doing.

1 Thessalonians 5:11 HCSB

I want their hearts to be encouraged and joined together in love, so that they may have all the riches of assured understanding, and have the knowledge of God's mystery—Christ.

Colossians 2:2 HCSB

Carry one another's burdens; in this way you will fulfill the law of Christ.

Galatians 6:2 HCSB

123

BE ENCOURAGING

Spend a few minutes writing some encouraging thoughts you'd like to hear or to say to your friends.

_____

_____

_____

_____

_____

_____

_____

_____

_____

_____

_____

OUT

SOME BIG IDEAS

We can never untangle all the woes in other people's lives. We can't produce miracles overnight. But we can bring a cup of cool water to a thirsty soul, or a scoop of laughter to a lonely heart.

Barbara Johnson

How many people stop because so few say, "Go!"

Charles Swindoll

God grant that we may not hinder those who are battling their way slowly into the light.

Oswald Chambers

A single word, if spoken in a friendly spirit, may be sufficient to turn one from dangerous error.

Fanny Crosby

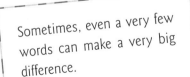

Sometimes, even a very few words can make a very big difference.

CONTAGIOUS FAITH

Whatever you do, do it enthusiastically, as something done for the Lord and not for men.

Colossians 3:23 HCSB

The stronger your faith, the better you can rise above the inevitable stresses of everyday life. And the more enthused you are about your faith, the better you can share it.

Are you genuinely excited about your faith? And do you make your enthusiasm known to those around you? Or are you a "silent ambassador" for Christ? God's preference is clear: He intends that you stand before others and proclaim your faith.

Genuine, heartfelt Christianity is contagious. If you enjoy a life-altering relationship with God, that relationship will have an impact on others—perhaps a profound impact.

Does Christ reign over your life? Then share your testimony and your excitement. The world needs both.

MORE FROM GOD'S WORD

Never be lazy in your work, but serve the Lord enthusiastically.

Romans 12:11 NLT

Whatever work you do, do your best, because you are going to the grave, where there is no working . . . .

Ecclesiastes 9:10 NCV

I have seen that there is nothing better than for a person to enjoy his activities, because that is his reward. For who can enable him to see what will happen after he dies?

Ecclesiastes 3:22 HCSB

Do your work with enthusiasm. Work as if you were serving the Lord, not as if you were serving only men and women.

Ephesians 6:7 NCV

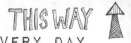
SOME BIG IDEAS

We act as though comfort and luxury were the chief requirements of life, when all we need to make us really happy is something to be enthusiastic about.

Charles Kingsley

Your enthusiasm will be infectious, stimulating, and attractive to others. They will love you for it. They will go for you and with you.

Norman Vincent Peale

Don't take hold of a thing unless you want that thing to take hold of you.

E. Stanley Jones

Remember, a small light will do a great deal when it is in a very dark place. Put one little tallow candle in the middle of a large hall, and it will give a great deal of light.

D. L. Moody

Make certain that your candle is always lit. Give your testimony, and trust God to do the rest.

FINDING PEACE

These things I have spoken to you, that in Me you may have peace. In the world you will have tribulation; but be of good cheer, I have overcome the world.

John 16:33 NKJV

Oftentimes, our outer struggles are simply manifestations of the inner conflict that we feel when we stray from God's path. Jesus offers us peace, not as the world gives, but as He alone gives. Our challenge is to accept Christ's peace into our hearts and then, as best we can, to share His peace with our neighbors. When we accept Jesus as our personal Savior, we are transformed by His grace. We are then free to accept the spiritual abundance and peace that can be ours through the power of the risen Christ.

Have you found the genuine peace that can be yours through Jesus Christ? Or are you still rushing after the illusion of "peace and happiness" that the world promises but cannot deliver? Today, as a gift to yourself, to your family, and to your friends, claim the

inner peace that is your spiritual birthright: the peace of Jesus Christ. It is offered freely; it has been paid for in full; it is yours for the asking. So ask. And then share.

MORE FROM GOD'S WORD

God has called us to peace.

1 Corinthians 7:15 NKJV

Live peaceful and quiet lives in all godliness and holiness.

1 Timothy 2:2 NIV

You, Lord, give true peace to those who depend on you, because they trust you.

Isaiah 26:3 NCV

And the peace of God, which transcends all understanding, will guard your hearts and your minds in Christ Jesus.

Philippians 4:7 NIV

OUT

SOME BIG IDEAS

Prayer guards hearts and minds and causes God to bring peace out of chaos.

Beth Moore

The fruit of our placing all things in God's hands is the presence of His abiding peace in our hearts.

Hannah Whitall Smith

> Do you want to discover God's peace? Then do your best to live in the center of God's will.

When we do what is right, we have contentment, peace, and happiness.

Beverly LaHaye

To know God as He really is—in His essential nature and character—is to arrive at a citadel of peace that circumstances may storm, but can never capture.

Catherine Marshall

NEXT

AVOID THE WRONG KIND OF PEER PRESSURE

Whoever walks with the wise will become wise; whoever walks with fools will suffer harm.

Proverbs 13:20 NLT

Who you are depends, to a surprising extent, on the people you hang out with. Peer pressure can be good or bad, depending upon who your peers are and how they behave. If your friends encourage you to follow God's will and to obey His commandments, then you'll experience positive peer pressure, and that's a good thing. But, if your friends encourage you to do foolish things, then you're facing a different kind of peer pressure . . . and you'd better beware.

Do you want to feel good about yourself and your life? If so, here's a simple, proven strategy: go out and find friends who, by their words and their actions, will help you build the kind of life that's worth feeling good about.

MORE FROM GOD'S WORD

Do not be misled: "Bad company corrupts good character."

1 Corinthians 15:33 NIV

Don't become partners with those who reject God. How can you make a partnership out of right and wrong? That's not partnership; that's war. Is light best friends with dark?

2 Corinthians 6:14 MSG

Friend, don't go along with evil. Model the good. The person who does good does God's work. The person who does evil falsifies God, doesn't know the first thing about God.

3 John 1:11 MSG

We must obey God rather than men.

Acts 5:29 HCSB

NEXT

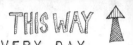

SOME BIG IDEAS

Nothing can be more dangerous than keeping wicked companions. They communicate the infection of their vices to all who associate with them.

St. Jean Baptiste de la Salle

If you're hanging out with friends who behave badly, you're heading straight for trouble. To avoid negative consequences, pick friends who avoid negative behaviors.

Choose the opposition of the whole world rather than offend Jesus.

Thomas à Kempis

You'll probably end up behaving like your friends behave . . . and if that's a scary thought, it time to make a new set of friends.

Criswell Freeman

When we are set free from the bondage of pleasing others, when we are free from currying others' favor and others' approval—then no one will be able to make us miserable or dissatisfied. And then, if we know we have pleased God, contentment will be our consolation.

Kay Arthur

GOOD DECISIONS
PAY BIG DIVIDENDS

If you need wisdom—if you want to know what God wants you to do—ask him, and he will gladly tell you. He will not resent your asking.

James 1:5 NLT

Everyday life is an adventure in decision-making. Each day, we make countless decisions that hopefully bring us closer to God. When we obey God's commandments, we share in His abundance and His peace. But, when we turn our backs upon God by disobeying Him, we invite Old Man Trouble stop by for an extended visit.

Do you want to be successful and happy? If so, here's a good place to start: Obey God. When you're faced with a difficult choice or a powerful temptation, pray about it. Invite God into your heart and live according to His commandments. When you do, you will be blessed today, and tomorrow, and forever.

MORE FROM GOD'S WORD

The thing you should want most is God's kingdom and doing what God wants. Then all these other things you need will be given to you.

Matthew 6:33 NCV

Above all and before all, do this: Get Wisdom! Write this at the top of your list: Get Understanding!

Proverbs 4:7 MSG

Even zeal is not good without knowledge, and the one who acts hastily sins.

Proverbs 19:2 HCSB

Give instruction to a wise man, and he will be still wiser; Teach a just man, and he will increase in learning.

Proverbs 9:9 NKJV

SOME BIG IDEAS

If we don't hunger and thirst after righteousness, we'll become anemic and feel miserable in our Christian experience.

Franklin Graham

Righteousness not only defines God, but God defines righteousness.

Bill Hybels

Life is built on character, but character is built on decisions.

Warren Wiersbe

The Reference Point for the Christian is the Bible. All values, judgments, and attitudes must be gauged in relationship to this Reference Point.

Ruth Bell Graham

Slow down! If you're about to make an important decision, don't be impulsive. Big decisions have big consequences, and if you don't think about those consequences now, you may pay a big price later.

137

GOD ANSWERS
PRAYERS

If you believe, you will receive whatever you ask for in prayer.

Matthew 21:22 NIV

In case you've been wondering, wonder no more—God does answer your prayers. What God does not do is this: He does not always answer your prayers as soon as you might like, and He does not always answer your prayers by saying "Yes."

God isn't an order-taker, and He's not some sort of cosmic vending machine. Sometimes—even when we want something very badly—our loving Heavenly Father responds to our requests by saying "No," and we must accept His answer, even if we don't understand it.

God answers prayers not only according to our wishes but also according to His master plan. We cannot know that plan, but we can know the Planner . . . and we must trust His wisdom, His righteousness, and His love.

Of this you can be sure: God is listening, and He wants to hear from you now. So what are you waiting for?

MORE FROM GOD'S WORD

The intense prayer of the righteous is very powerful.

James 5:16 HCSB

Rejoice in hope; be patient in affliction; be persistent in prayer.

Romans 12:12 HCSB

Don't worry about anything, but in everything, through prayer and petition with thanksgiving, let your requests be made known to God.

Philippians 4:6 HCSB

Ask, and it shall be given you; seek, and ye shall find; knock, and it shall be opened unto you: for every one that asketh receiveth; and he that seeketh findeth; and to him that knocketh it shall be opened.

Matthew 7:7-8 KJV

NEXT

THE POWER OF PRAYER

Take a few minutes and write down some things or some people you need to pray for in the boxes below.

OUT

SOME BIG IDEAS

Avail yourself of the greatest privilege this side of heaven: prayer. Jesus Christ died to make this communion and communication with the Father possible.

Billy Graham

Are you weak? Weary? Confused? Troubled? Pressured? How is your relationship with God? Is it held in its place of priority? I believe the greater the pressure, the greater your need for time alone with Him.

Kay Arthur

If something is important to you, it's important to God, so go ahead and tell God what hurts. Talk to him. He won't turn you away. He won't think it's silly. Does God care about the little things in our lives? You better believe it. If it matters to you, it matters to him.

Max Lucado

> Pray early and often. One way to make sure that your heart is in tune with God is to pray often. The more you talk to God, the more He will talk to you.

141

GOD IS SUFFICIENT TO MEET YOUR NEEDS

The Lord is my rock, my fortress, and my deliverer.
Psalm 18:2 HCSB

It is easy to become overwhelmed by the demands of everyday life, but if you're a faithful follower of the One from Galilee, you need never be overwhelmed. Why? Because God's love is sufficient to meet your needs. Whatever dangers you may face, whatever heartbreaks you must endure, God is with you, and He stands ready to comfort you and to heal you.

The Psalmist writes, "Weeping may endure for a night, but joy comes in the morning" (Psalm 30:5 NKJV). But when we are suffering, the morning may seem very far away. It is not. God promises that He is "near to those who have a broken heart" (Psalm 34:18 NKJV).

If you are experiencing the intense pain of a recent loss, or if you are still mourning a loss from long ago, perhaps you are now ready to begin the next stage of

your journey with God. If so, be mindful of this fact: the loving heart of God is sufficient to meet any challenge, including yours.

MORE FROM GOD'S WORD

Now the God of all grace, who called you to His eternal glory in Christ Jesus, will personally restore, establish, strengthen, and support you.

1 Peter 5:10 HCSB

Peace, peace to you, and peace to your helpers! For your God helps you.

1 Chronicles 12:18 NKJV

The LORD is my strength and song, and He has become my salvation; He is my God, and I will praise Him…

Exodus 15:2 NKJV

Therefore whoever hears these sayings of Mine, and does them, I will liken him to a wise man who built his house on the rock: and the rain descended, the floods came, and the winds blew and beat on that house; and it did not fall, for it was founded on the rock.

Matthew 7:24-25 NKJV

NEXT

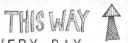

SOME BIG IDEAS

God is, must be, our answer to every question and every cry of need.

Hannah Whitall Smith

God will call you to obey Him and do whatever he asks of you. However, you do not need to be doing something to feel fulfilled. You are fulfilled completely in a relationship with God. When you are filled with Him, what else do you need?

Henry Blackaby and Claude King

Faith is not merely you holding on to God—it is God holding on to you.

E. Stanley Jones

Focus on possibilities, not stumbling blocks. You will encounter occasional disappointments, and, from time to time, you will encounter failure. But, don't invest large quantities of your life focusing on past misfortunes. Instead, look to the future with optimism and hope.

DEVO 45

A GOOD ATTITUDE
PAYS BIG REWARDS

Finally brothers, whatever is true, whatever is honorable, whatever is just, whatever is pure, whatever is lovely, whatever is commendable—if there is any moral excellence and if there is any praise—dwell on these things.

Philippians 4:8 HCSB

How will you direct your thoughts today? Will you obey the words of Philippians 4:8 by dwelling upon those things that are honorable, just, and commendable? Or will you allow your thoughts to be hijacked by the negativity that seems to dominate our troubled world? Are you fearful, angry, stressed, or worried? Are you so preoccupied with the concerns of this day that you fail to thank God for the promise of eternity? Are you confused, bitter, or pessimistic? If so, God wants to have a little talk with you.

God intends that you experience joy and abundance. So, today and every day hereafter, celebrate the

FOLLOWING HIM EVERY DAY

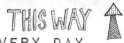
life that God has given you by focusing your thoughts upon those things that are worthy of praise. Today, count your blessings instead of your hardships. And thank the Giver of all things good for gifts that are simply too numerous to count.

MORE FROM GOD'S WORD

For the word of God is living and effective and sharper than any two-edged sword, penetrating as far as to divide soul, spirit, joints, and marrow; it is a judge of the ideas and thoughts of the heart.

Hebrews 4:12 HCSB

Make your own attitude that of Christ Jesus.

Philippians 2:5 HCSB

Set your minds on what is above, not on what is on the earth.

Colossians 3:2 HCSB

A cheerful heart has a continual feast.

Proverbs 15:15 HCSB

SOME BIG IDEAS

The mind is like a clock that is constantly running down. It has to be wound up daily with good thoughts.

Fulton J. Sheen

I could go through this day oblivious to the miracles all around me, or I could tune in and "enjoy."

Gloria Gaither

The things we think are the things that feed our souls. If we think on pure and lovely things, we shall grow pure and lovely like them; and the converse is equally true.

Hannah Whitall Smith

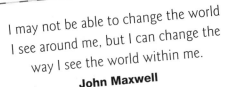

I may not be able to change the world I see around me, but I can change the way I see the world within me.

John Maxwell

GOD WILL RENEW YOUR STRENGTH

He gives strength to the weary and strengthens the powerless.

Isaiah 40:29 HCSB

When we genuinely lift our hearts and prayers to God, He renews our strength. Are you almost too stressed to lift your head? Then bow it. Offer your concerns and your fears to your Father in Heaven. He is always at your side, offering His love and His strength.

Are you troubled or anxious? Take your anxieties to God in prayer. Are you weak or worried? Delve deeply into God's Holy Word and sense His presence in the quiet moments of the day. Are you spiritually exhausted? Call upon fellow believers to support you, and call upon Christ to renew your spirit and your life. Your Savior will never let you down. To the contrary, He will always lift you up if you ask Him to. So what, dear friend, are you waiting for?

MORE FROM GOD'S WORD

The One who was sitting on the throne said, "Look! I am making everything new!" Then he said, "Write this, because these words are true and can be trusted."

Revelation 21:5 NCV

When doubts filled my mind, your comfort gave me renewed hope and cheer.

Psalm 94:19 NLT

Create in me a pure heart, O God, and renew a steadfast spirit within me. Do not cast me from your presence or take your Holy Spirit from me. Restore to me the joy of your salvation and grant me a willing spirit, to sustain me.

Psalm 51:10-12 NIV

Finally, brothers, rejoice. Be restored, be encouraged, be of the same mind, be at peace, and the God of love and peace will be with you.

2 Corinthians 13:11 HCSB

SOME BIG IDEAS

He is the God of wholeness and restoration.

Stormie Omartian

> If you're energy is low or your nerves are frazzled, perhaps you need to slow down and have a heart-to-heart talk with God. And while you're at it, remember that God is bigger than your problems . . . much bigger.

Repentance removes old sins and wrong attitudes, and it opens the way for the Holy Spirit to restore our spiritual health.

Shirley Dobson

God gives us permission to forget our past and the understanding to live our present. He said He will remember our sins no more. (Psalm 103:11-12)

Serita Ann Jakes

When we reach the end of our strength, wisdom, and personal resources, we enter into the beginning of his glorious provisions.

Patsy Clairmont

TRUST YOUR FUTURE TO GOD

"I say this because I know what I am planning for you,"
says the Lord. "I have good plans for you, not plans to
hurt you. I will give you hope and a good future."

Jeremiah 29:11 NCV

How can you make smart choices if you're unwilling to trust God and obey Him? The answer, of course, is that you can't. That's why you should trust God in everything (and that means entrusting your future to God).

How bright is your future? Well, if you're a faithful believer, God's plans for you are so bright that you'd better wear shades. Here are some important follow-up questions: How bright do you believe your future to be? Are you expecting a terrific tomorrow, or are you dreading a terrible one? The answer you give will have a powerful impact on the way tomorrow turns out.

Do you trust in the ultimate goodness of God's plan for your life? Will you face tomorrow's challenges

with optimism and hope? You should. After all, God created you for a very important reason: His reason. And you have important work to do: His work.

Today, as you live in the present and look to the future, remember that God has an amazing plan for you. Act—and believe—accordingly.

MORE FROM GOD'S WORD

Do not boast about tomorrow, for you do not know what a day may bring forth.

Proverbs 27:1 NKJV

For now we see indistinctly, as in a mirror, but then face to face. Now I know in part, but then I will know fully, as I am fully known.

1 Corinthians 13:12 HCSB

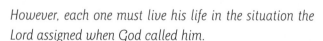

However, each one must live his life in the situation the Lord assigned when God called him.

1 Corinthians 7:17 HCSB

OUT

SOME BIG IDEAS

We must trust as if it all depended on God and work as if it all depended on us.

C. H. Spurgeon

Every man lives by faith, the nonbeliever as well as the saint; the one by faith in natural laws and the other by faith in God.

A. W. Tozer

Faith in faith is pointless. Faith in a living, active God moves mountains.

Beth Moore

The Christian believes in a fabulous future.

Billy Graham

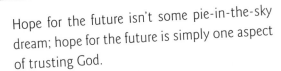

Hope for the future isn't some pie-in-the-sky dream; hope for the future is simply one aspect of trusting God.

153

BEYOND ENVY

Therefore, laying aside all malice, all deceit, hypocrisy, envy, and all evil speaking, as newborn babes, desire the pure milk of the word, that you may grow thereby.

1 Peter 2:1-2 NKJV

Because we are frail, imperfect human beings, we are sometimes envious of others. But God's Word warns us that envy is sin. Thus, we must guard ourselves against the natural tendency to feel resentment and jealousy when other people experience good fortune. As believers, we have absolutely no reason to be envious of any people on earth. After all, as Christians we are already recipients of the greatest gift in all creation: God's grace. We have been promised the gift of eternal life through God's only begotten Son, and we must count that gift as our most precious possession.

So here's a simple suggestion that is guaranteed to bring you happiness: fill your heart with God's love, God's promises, and God's Son . . . and when you do so, leave no room for envy, hatred, bitterness, or regret.

MORE FROM GOD'S WORD

Do not covet your neighbor's house . . . or anything that belongs to your neighbor.

Exodus 20:17 HCSB

Stop your anger! Turn from your rage! Do not envy others—it only leads to harm.

Psalm 37:8 NLT

We must not become conceited, provoking one another, envying one another.

Galatians 5:26 HCSB

If your sinful nature controls your mind, there is death. But if the Holy Spirit controls your mind, there is life and peace.

Romans 8:6 NLT

155

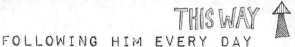
SOME BIG IDEAS

How can you possess the miseries of envy when you possess in Christ the best of all portions?

C. H. Spurgeon

Is there somebody who's always getting your goat? Talk to the Shepherd.

Anonymous

Envy is a sin, a sin that robs you of contentment and peace. So you must stead-fastly refuse to let feelings of envy invade your thoughts or your heart.

What God asks, does, or requires of others is not my business; it is His.

Kay Arthur

Discontent dries up the soul.

Elisabeth Elliot

BEING A GOOD EXAMPLE

*For am I now trying to win the favor of people, or God?
Or am I striving to please people? If I were still trying to
please people, I would not be a slave of Christ.*

Galatians 1:10 HCSB

Whether you like it or not, you simply can't deny the fact that you're an example to other people. The question is not whether you will be an example to your family and friends; the question is precisely what kind of example will you be.

Corrie ten Boom advised, "Don't worry about what you do not understand. Worry about what you do understand in the Bible but do not live by." And that's sound advice because your family and friends are always watching . . . and so, for that matter, is God.

MORE FROM GOD'S WORD

In every way be an example of doing good deeds. When you teach, do it with honesty and seriousness.

Titus 2:7 NCV

In everything you do, stay away from complaining and arguing, so that no one can speak a word of blame against you. You are to live clean, innocent lives as children of God in a dark world full of crooked and perverse people. Let your lives shine brightly before them.

Philippians 2:14-15 NLT

You are the light that gives light to the world. In the same way, you should be a light for other people. Live so that they will see the good things you do and will praise your Father in heaven.

Matthew 5:14, 16 NCV

You should be an example to the believers in speech, in conduct, in love, in faith, in purity.

1 Timothy 4:12 HCSB

SOME BIG IDEAS

Too many Christians have geared their program to please, to entertain, and to gain favor from this world. We are concerned with how much, instead of how little, like this age we can become.

Billy Graham

Nothing speaks louder or more powerfully than a life of integrity.

Charles Swindoll

In your desire to share the gospel, you may be the only Jesus someone else will ever meet. Be real and be involved with people.

Barbara Johnson

> If you're a Christian, behave like one. The sermons you live are far more important than the sermons you preach.

We urgently need people who encourage and inspire us to move toward God and away from the world's enticing pleasures.

Jim Cymbala

EXPECT
HIS ABUNDANCE

I have come that they may have life, and that they may have it more abundantly.

John 10:10 NKJV

When Jesus talks of the abundant life, is He talking about material riches or earthly fame? Hardly. The Son of God came to this world, not to give it prosperity, but to give it salvation. Thankfully for Christians, our Savior's abundance is both spiritual and eternal; it never falters—even if we do—and it never dies. We need only to open our hearts to Him, and His grace becomes ours.

God's gifts are available to all, but they are not guaranteed; those gifts must be claimed by those who choose to follow Christ. As believers, we are free to accept God's gifts, or not; that choice, and the consequences that result from it, are ours and ours alone.

As we go about our daily lives, may we accept God's promise of spiritual abundance, and may we share it with a world in desperate need of the Master's healing touch.

MORE FROM GOD'S WORD

And God is able to make every grace overflow to you, so that in every way, always having everything you need, you may excel in every good work.

2 Corinthians 9:8 HCSB

Until now you have asked for nothing in My name. Ask and you will receive, that your joy may be complete.

John 16:24 HCSB

Come to terms with God and be at peace; in this way good will come to you.

Job 22:21 HCSB

My cup runs over. Surely goodness and mercy shall follow me all the days of my life; and I will dwell in the house of the Lord forever.

Psalm 23:5-6 NKJV

SOME BIG IDEAS

If we just give God the little that we have, we can trust Him to make it go around.

Gloria Gaither

If we were given all we wanted here, our hearts would settle for this world rather than the next.

Elisabeth Elliot

God is the giver, and we are the receivers. And His richest gifts are bestowed not upon those who do the greatest things, but upon those who accept His abundance and His grace.

Hannah Whitall Smith

Abundant living may or may not include material wealth, but abundant living always includes the spiritual riches that you receive when you obey God's Word.

BITTERNESS PUTS DISTANCE BETWEEN YOU AND GOD

All bitterness, anger and wrath, insult and slander must be removed from you, along with all wickedness. And be kind and compassionate to one another, forgiving one another, just as God also forgave you in Christ.

Ephesians 4:31-32 HCSB

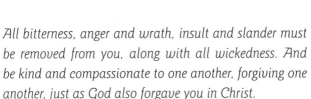

If you're unwilling to forgive other people, you're building a roadblock between yourself and God. And the less you're willing to forgive, the bigger your roadblock. So if you want to know God in a more meaningful way, you must learn how to forgive and, to the best of your abilities, forget.

Is there someone out there you need to forgive? If so, pray for that person. And then pray for yourself by asking God to heal your heart. Don't expect forgiveness to be easy or quick, but rest assured: with God as your partner, you can forgive . . . and you will.

MORE FROM GOD'S WORD

Don't insist on getting even; that's not for you to do. "I'll do the judging," says God. "I'll take care of it."

Romans 12:19 MSG

But now you must also put away all the following: anger, wrath, malice, slander, and filthy language from your mouth.

Colossians 3:8 HCSB

When you are angry, do not sin, and be sure to stop being angry before the end of the day. Do not give the devil a way to defeat you.

Ephesians 4:26–27 NCV

See to it that no one repays evil for evil to anyone, but always pursue what is good for one another and for all.

1 Thessalonians 5:15 HCSB

SOME BIG IDEAS

By not forgiving, by not letting wrongs go, we aren't getting back at anyone. We are merely punishing ourselves by barricading our own hearts.

Jim Cymbala

Forgiveness enables you to bury your grudge in icy earth. To put the past behind you. To flush resentment away by being the first to forgive. Forgiveness fashions your future. It is a brave and brash thing to do.

Barbara Johnson

Bitterness is a spiritual cancer, a rapidly growing malignancy that can consume your life. Bitterness cannot be ignored but must be healed at the very core, and only Christ can heal bitterness.

Beth Moore

Jesus had a loving heart. If he dwells within us, hatred and bitterness will never rule us.

Billy Graham

IT PAYS TO BE A CHEERFUL CHRISTIAN

A cheerful heart has a continual feast.

Proverbs 15:15 HCSB

Few things in life are more sad, or, for that matter, more absurd, than a grumpy Christian. Christ promises us lives of abundance and joy, but He does not force His joy upon us. We must claim His joy for ourselves, and when we do, Jesus, in turn, fills our spirits with His power and His love.

How can we receive from Christ the joy that is rightfully ours? By giving Him what is rightfully His: our hearts and our souls.

When we earnestly commit ourselves to the Savior of mankind, when we place Jesus at the center of our lives and trust Him as our personal Savior, He will transform us, not just for today, but for all eternity. Then we, as God's children, can share Christ's joy and His message with a world that needs both.

MORE FROM GOD'S WORD

Is anyone cheerful? He should sing praises.

James 5:13 HCSB

Make me hear joy and gladness.

Psalm 51:8 NKJV

Be cheerful. Keep things in good repair. Keep your spirits up. Think in harmony. Be agreeable. Do all that, and the God of love and peace will be with you for sure.

2 Corinthians 13:11 MSG

A cheerful heart is good medicine. . . .

Proverbs 17:22 NIV

Do you need a little cheering up? If so, find somebody else who needs cheering up, too. Then, do your best to brighten that person's day. When you do, you'll discover that cheering up other people is a wonderful way to cheer yourself up, too!

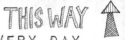

SOME BIG IDEAS

Be assured, my dear friend, that it is no joy to God in seeing you with a dreary countenance.

C. H. Spurgeon

Sour godliness is the devil's religion.

John Wesley

The people whom I have seen succeed best in life have always been cheerful and hopeful people who went about their business with a smile on their faces.

Charles Kingsley

Christ can put a spring in your step and a thrill in your heart. Optimism and cheerfulness are products of knowing Christ.

Billy Graham

TOUGH TIMES HAVE LESSONS TO TEACH

If you hide your sins, you will not succeed. If you confess and reject them, you will receive mercy.

Proverbs 28:13 NCV

Everybody makes mistakes, and so will you. In fact, Winston Churchill once observed, "Success is going from failure to failure without loss of enthusiasm." What was good for Churchill is also good for you. You should expect to make mistakes—plenty of mistakes—but you should not allow those missteps to rob you of the enthusiasm you need to fulfill God's plan for your life.

We are imperfect people living in an imperfect world; mistakes are simply part of the price we pay for being here. But, even though mistakes are an inevitable part of life's journey, repeated mistakes should not be. When we commit the inevitable blunders of life, we must correct them, learn from them, and pray for the wisdom not to repeat them. When we do, our mistakes

become lessons, and our lives become adventures in growth, not stagnation.

Have you made a mistake or three? Of course you have. But here's the big question: have you used your mistakes as stumbling blocks or stepping stones? The answer to that question will determine how well you will perform in every aspect of your life.

MORE FROM GOD'S WORD

If you listen to constructive criticism, you will be at home among the wise.

Proverbs 15:31 NLT

If we confess our sins to him, he is faithful and just to forgive us and to cleanse us from every wrong.

1 John 1:9 NLT

Instead, God has chosen the world's foolish things to shame the wise, and God has chosen the world's weak things to shame the strong.

1 Corinthians 1:27 HCSB

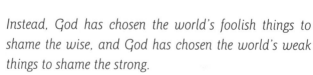

OUT

SOME BIG IDEAS

Mistakes offer the possibility for redemption and a new start in God's kingdom. No matter what you're guilty of, God can restore your innocence.

Barbara Johnson

Truth will sooner come out of error than from confusion.

Francis Bacon

Very few things motivate us to give God our undivided attention like being faced with the negative consequences of our decisions.

Charles Stanley

Lord, when we are wrong, make us willing to change; and when we are right, make us easy to live with.

Peter Marshall

> Fix it sooner rather than later: When you make a mistake, the time to make things better is now, not later! The sooner you address your problem, the less stress you'll have to endure.

NEGATIVITY IS A TRAP

Let angry people endure the backlash of their own anger; if you try to make it better, you'll only make it worse.

Proverbs 19:19 MSG

From experience, we know that it is easy to criticize others. And we know that it is usually far easier to find faults than to find solutions. Still, the urge to criticize others remains a powerful temptation for most of us.

Negativity is highly contagious: We give it to others who, in turn, give it back to us. This stress-inducing cycle can be broken only by positive thoughts, heart-felt prayers, encouraging words, and meaningful acts of kindness.

As thoughtful servants of a loving God, we have no valid reason—and no legitimate excuse—to be negative. So, when we are tempted to be overly critical of others, or unfairly critical of ourselves, we must use the

MORE FROM GOD'S WORD

Set your mind on things above, not on things on the earth.
Colossians 3:2 NKJV

*Those who are pure in their thinking are happy, because

Matthew 5:8 NCV

*But if we look forward to something we don't have yet,

Romans 8:25 NLT

Make me hear joy and gladness.

Psalm 51:8 NKJV

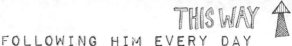

SOME BIG IDEAS

Winners see an answer for every problem; losers see a problem in every answer.

Barbara Johnson

We never get anywhere—nor do our conditions and circumstances change—when we look at the dark side of life.

Mrs. Charles E. Cowman

To lose heart is to lose everything.

John Eldredge

After one hour in heaven, we shall be ashamed that we ever grumbled.

Vance Havner

Negative thinking breeds more negative thinking, so nip negativity in the bud, starting today and continuing every day of your life.

IT PAYS TO BE PATIENT

Be gentle to everyone, able to teach, and patient.

2 Timothy 2:23 HCSB

Are you a perfectly patient person? If so, feel free to skip the rest of this page. But if you're not, here's something to think about: If you really want to become a more patient person, God is ready and willing to help.

The Bible promises that when you sincerely seek God's help, He will give you the things that you need—and that includes patience. But God won't force you to become a more patient person. If you want to become a more mature Christian, you've got to do some of the work yourself—and the best time to start doing that work is now.

So, if you want to gain patience and maturity, bow your head and start praying about it. Then, rest assured that with God's help, you can most certainly make yourself a more patient, understanding, mature Christian.

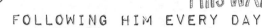

MORE FROM GOD'S WORD

Rejoice in hope; be patient in affliction; be persistent in prayer.

Romans 12:12 HCSB

Now we exhort you, brethren, warn those who are unruly, comfort the fainthearted, uphold the weak, be patient with all.

1 Thessalonians 5:14 NKJV

A patient spirit is better than a proud spirit.

Ecclesiastes 7:8 HCSB

Therefore the Lord is waiting to show you mercy, and is rising up to show you compassion, for the Lord is a just God. Happy are all who wait patiently for Him.

Isaiah 30:18 HCSB

SOME BIG IDEAS

Be patient. God is using today's difficulties to strengthen you for tomorrow. He is equipping you. The God who makes things grow will help you bear fruit.

Max Lucado

You can't step in front of God and not get in trouble. When He says, "Go three steps," don't go four.

Charles Stanley

The deepest spiritual lessons are not learned by His letting us have our way in the end, but by His making us wait, bearing with us in love and patience until we are able honestly to pray what He taught His disciples to pray: Thy will be done.

Elisabeth Elliot

Want other people to be patient with you? Then you must do the same for them. Never expect other people to be more patient with you than you are with them.

THINK AHEAD

I will instruct you and teach you in the way you should go; I will guide you with My eye.

Psalm 32:8 NKJV

Maybe you've heard this old saying: "Look before you leap." Well, that saying may be old, but it still applies to you. Before you jump into something, you should look ahead and plan ahead. Otherwise, you might soon be sorry you jumped!

When you acquire the habit of thinking ahead and planning ahead, you'll make better choices (and, as a result, you'll feel better about yourself).

So when it comes to the important things in life, don't allow impulsive behavior to dynamite your future. Think long and hard about the consequences of your actions before you do something foolish . . . or dangerous . . . or both.

MORE FROM GOD'S WORD

Enthusiasm without knowledge is not good. If you act too quickly, you might make a mistake.

Proverbs 19:2 NCV

The wise inherit honor, but fools are put to shame!

Proverbs 3:35 NLT

Grow a wise heart—you'll do yourself a favor; keep a clear head—you'll find a good life.

Proverbs 19:8 MSG

The one who walks with the wise will become wise, but a companion of fools will suffer harm.

Proverbs 13:20 HCSB

NEXT

179

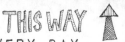
SOME BIG IDEAS

It's incredible to realize that what we do each day has meaning in the big picture of God's plan.

Bill Hybels

Allow your dreams a place in your prayers and plans. God-given dreams can help you move into the future He is preparing for you.

Barbara Johnson

The only way you can experience abundant life is to surrender your plans to Him.

Charles Stanley

Sometimes, being wise is nothing more than slowing down long enough to think about things before you do them.

Marie T. Freeman

Think ahead—it's the best way of making sure you don't get left behind.

USING YOUR GIFTS

I remind you to keep ablaze the gift of God that is in you.
2 Timothy 1:6 HCSB

How do we thank God for the gifts He has given us? By using those gifts, that's how!

God has given you talents and opportunities that are uniquely yours. Are you willing to use your gifts in the way that God intends? And are you willing to summon the discipline that is required to develop your talents and to hone your skills? That's precisely what God wants you to do, and that's precisely what you should desire for yourself.

As you seek to expand your talents, you will undoubtedly encounter stumbling blocks along the way, such as the fear of rejection or the fear of failure. When you do, don't stumble! Just continue to refine your skills, and offer your services to God. And when the time is right, He will use you—but it's up to you to be thoroughly prepared when He does.

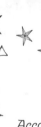
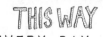

MORE FROM GOD'S WORD

According to the grace given to us, we have different gifts: If prophecy, use it according to the standard of faith; if service, in service; if teaching, in teaching; if exhorting, in exhortation; giving, with generosity; leading, with diligence; showing mercy, with cheerfulness.

Romans 12:6-8 HCSB

Every generous act and every perfect gift is from above, coming down from the Father of lights.

James 1:17 HCSB

Based on the gift they have received, everyone should use it to serve others, as good managers of the varied grace of God.

1 Peter 4:10 HCSB

Now there are different gifts, but the same Spirit. There are different ministries, but the same Lord.

1 Corinthians 12:4-5 HCSB

SOME BIG IDEAS

You are the only person on earth who can use your ability.

Zig Ziglar

God often reveals His direction for our lives through the way He made us . . . with a certain personality and unique skills.

Bill Hybels

The Lord has abundantly blessed me all of my life. I'm not trying to pay Him back for all of His wonderful gifts; I just realize that He gave them to me to give away.

Lisa Whelchel

God has given you special talents—now it's your turn to give them back to God.

Marie T. Freeman

God has given you a unique array of talents and opportunities. If you use your gifts wisely, they're multiplied. If you misuse your gifts—or ignore them altogether— they are lost. God is anxious for you to use your gifts . . . are you?

PUT GOD FIRST

You shall have no other gods before Me.

Exodus 20:3 NKJV

Who is in charge of your heart? Is it God, or is it something else? Have you given Christ your heart, your soul, your talents, your time, and your testimony? Or are you giving Him little more than a few hours each Sunday morning?

In the book of Exodus, God warns that we should place no gods before Him. Yet all too often, we place our Lord in second, third, or fourth place as we worship other things. When we unwittingly place possessions or relationships above our love for the Creator, we create big problems for ourselves.

Have you chosen to allow God to rule your heart? Make certain that the honest answer to this question is a resounding yes. In the life of every thoughtful believer, God comes first. And that's precisely the place that He deserves in your heart.

MORE FROM GOD'S WORD

Be careful not to forget the Lord.

Deuteronomy 6:12 HCSB

It is good to give thanks to the Lord, and to sing praises to Your name, O Most High; to declare Your lovingkindness in the morning, and Your faithfulness every night.

Psalm 92:1-2 NKJV

Love the Lord your God with all your heart, with all your soul, and with all your strength.

Deuteronomy 6:5 HCSB

The Devil said to Him, "I will give You their splendor and all this authority, because it has been given over to me, and I can give it to anyone I want. If You, then, will worship me, all will be Yours." And Jesus answered him, "It is written: You shall worship the Lord your God, and Him alone you shall serve."

Luke 4:6-8 HCSB

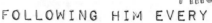
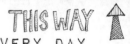

SOME BIG IDEAS

One with God is a majority.

Billy Graham

God is the beyond in the midst of our life.

Dietrich Bonhoeffer

You can't get second things by putting them first; you can get second things only by putting first things first.

C. S. Lewis

We become whatever we are committed to.

Rick Warren

If you don't choose to put God first, you're making a bad choice.

GOD IS LOVE

God is love, and the one who remains in love remains in God, and God remains in him.

1 John 4:16 HCSB

The Bible makes this promise: God is love. It's a sweeping statement, a profoundly important description of what God is and how God works. God's love is perfect. When we open our hearts to His perfect love, we are touched by the Creator's hand, and we are transformed.

Today, even if you can only carve out a few quiet moments, offer sincere prayers of thanksgiving to your Creator. He loves you now and throughout all eternity. Open your heart to His presence and His love.

MORE FROM GOD'S WORD

Whoever is wise will observe these things, and they will understand the lovingkindness of the Lord.

Psalm 107:43 NKJV

For the Lord is good, and His love is eternal; His faithfulness endures through all generations.

Psalm 100:5 HCSB

Draw near to God, and He will draw near to you.

James 4:8 HCSB

For He is gracious and compassionate, slow to anger, rich in faithful love.

Joel 2:13 HCSB

Remember: God's love for you is too big to understand with your brain . . . but it's not too big to feel with your heart.

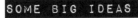

SOME BIG IDEAS

The life of faith is a daily exploration of the constant and countless ways in which God's grace and love are experienced.

Eugene Peterson

If you have an obedience problem, you have a love problem. Focus your attention on God's love.

Henry Blackaby

I can tell you, from personal experience of walking with God for over fifty years, that He is the Lover of my soul.

Vonette Bright

God loves these people too, just because they're unattractive or warped in their thinking doesn't mean the Lord doesn't love them.

Ruth Bell Graham

TRUST GOD'S PROMISES

God—His way is perfect; the word of the Lord is pure. He is a shield to all who take refuge in Him.

Psalm 18:30 HCSB

God has made quite a few promises to you, and He intends to keep every single one of them. You will find these promises in a book like no other: the Holy Bible. The Bible is your roadmap for life here on earth and for life eternal—as a believer, you are called upon to trust its promises, to follow its commandments, and to share its Good News.

God has made promises to all of humanity and to you. God's promises never fail and they never grow old. You must trust those promises and share them with your family, with your friends, and with the world . . . starting now . . . and ending never.

MORE FROM GOD'S WORD

Let us hold on to the confession of our hope without wavering, for He who promised is faithful.

Hebrews 10:23 HCSB

God also bound himself with an oath, so that those who received the promise could be perfectly sure that he would never change his mind. So God has given us both his promise and his oath. These two things are unchangeable because it is impossible for God to lie. Therefore, we who have fled to him for refuge can take new courage, for we can hold on to his promise with confidence.

Hebrews 6:17-18 NLT

Patient endurance is what you need now, so you will continue to do God's will. Then you will receive all that he has promised.

Hebrews 10:36 NLT

Whatever God has promised gets stamped with the Yes of Jesus. In him, this is what we preach and pray, the great Amen, God's Yes and our Yes together, gloriously evident.

2 Corinthians 1:20 MSG

SOME BIG IDEAS

God's promises are medicine for the broken heart. Let Him comfort you. And, after He has comforted you, try to share that comfort with somebody else. It will do both of you good.

Warren Wiersbe

We cannot rely on God's promises without obeying His commandments.

John Calvin

The stars may fall, but God's promises will stand and be fulfilled.

J. I. Packer

There are four words I wish we would never forget, and they are, "God keeps his word."

Charles Swindoll

The promises of Scripture are not mere pious hopes or sanctified guesses. They are more than sentimental words to be printed on decorated cards for Sunday School children. They are eternal verities. They are true. There is no perhaps about them.

Peter Marshall

THE ULTIMATE ARMOR

If God is for us, who can be against us?

Romans 8:31 NIV

God has promised to protect us, and He intends to keep His promise. In a world filled with dangers and temptations, God is the ultimate armor. In a world filled with misleading messages, God's Word is the ultimate truth. In a world filled with more frustrations than we can count, God's Son offers the ultimate peace.

Will you accept God's peace and wear God's armor against the dangers of our world? Hopefully so, because when you do, you can live courageously, knowing that you possess the ultimate protection: God's unfailing love for you.

MORE FROM GOD'S WORD

Finally, my brethren, be strong in the Lord and in the power of His might. Put on the whole armor of God, that you may be able to stand against the wiles of the devil.

Ephesians 6:10-11 NKJV

The Lord your God in your midst, The Mighty One, will save; He will rejoice over you with gladness, He will quiet you with His love, He will rejoice over you with singing.

Zephaniah 3:17 NKJV

God is my shield, saving those whose hearts are true and right.

Psalm 7:10 NLT

But the Lord will be a refuge for His people.

Joel 3:16 HCSB

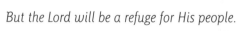

SOME BIG IDEAS

Under heaven's lock and key, we are protected by the most efficient security system available: the power of God.

Charles Swindoll

The Rock of Ages is the great sheltering encirclement.

Oswald Chambers

He goes before us, follows behind us, and hems us safe inside the realm of His protection.

Beth Moore

The Will of God will never take you where the Grace of God will not protect you.

Anonymous

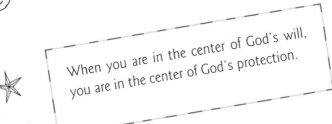

When you are in the center of God's will, you are in the center of God's protection.

WHO RULES?

Can you understand the secrets of God? His limits are higher than the heavens; you cannot reach them! They are deeper than the grave; you cannot understand them! His limits are longer than the earth and wider than the sea.

Job 11:7-9 NCV

God reigns over the entire universe and He reigns over your little corner of that universe. He is sovereign. Your challenge is to recognize God's sovereignty and live in accordance with His command-ments. Sometimes, of course, this is easier said than done.

Your Heavenly Father may not always reveal Him-self as quickly (or as clearly) as you would like. But rest assured: God is in control, God is here, and God intends to use you in wonderful, unexpected ways. He desires to lead you along a path of His choosing. Your challenge is to watch, to listen, to learn . . . and to follow.

MORE FROM GOD'S WORD

For now we see indistinctly, as in a mirror, but then face to face. Now I know in part, but then I will know fully, as I am fully known.

1 Corinthians 13:12 HCSB

However, each one must live his life in the situation the Lord assigned when God called him.

1 Corinthians 7:17 HCSB

O Lord, you have examined my heart and know everything about me. You know when I sit down or stand up. You know my every thought when far away. You chart the path ahead of me and tell me where to stop and rest.

Psalm 139:1-3 NLT

I am holding you by your right hand—I, the LORD your God. And I say to you, "Do not be afraid. I am here to help you . . ."

Isaiah 41:13 NLT

SOME BIG IDEAS

Our God is the sovereign Creator of the universe! He loves us as His own children and has provided every good thing we have; He is worthy of our praise every moment.

Shirley Dobson

The next time you're disappointed, don't panic. Don't give up. Just be patient and let God remind you he's still in control.

Max Lucado

God is in control, and therefore in everything I can give thanks, not because of the situation, but because of the One who directs and rules over it.

Kay Arthur

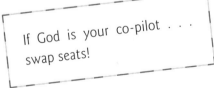

If God is your co-pilot . . . swap seats!

PROBLEM-SOLVING 101

People who do what is right may have many problems,
but the Lord will solve them all.

Psalm 34:19 NCV

L ife is an adventure in problem-solving. When it comes to solving the problems of everyday living, we often know precisely what needs to be done, but we may be slow in doing it—especially if what needs to be done is difficult. So we put off till tomorrow what should be done today.

As a young person living here in the 21st century, you have your own set of challenges. As you face those challenges, you may be comforted by this fact: Trouble, of every kind, is temporary. Yet God's grace is eternal. And worries, of every kind, are temporary. But God's love is everlasting. The troubles that concern you will pass. God remains. And for every problem, God has a solution.

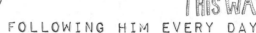

The words of Psalm 34 remind us that the Lord solves problems for "people who do what is right." And usually, doing "what is right" means doing the uncomfortable work of confronting our problems sooner rather than later. So with no further ado, let the problem-solving begin . . . right now.

MORE FROM GOD'S WORD

Come to me, all you who are weary and burdened, and I will give you rest. Take my yoke upon you and learn from me, for I am gentle and humble in heart, and you will find rest for your souls. For my yoke is easy and my burden is light.

Matthew 11:28-30 NIV

Be of good courage, and he shall strengthen your heart, all ye that hope in the LORD.

Psalm 31:24 KJV

Cast your burden on the Lord, and He will support you; He will never allow the righteous to be shaken.

Psalm 55:22 HCSB

SOME BIG IDEAS

Each problem is a God-appointed instructor.

Charles Swindoll

Life will be made or broken at the place where we meet and deal with obstacles.

E. Stanley Jones

Keep your feet on the ground, but let your heart soar as high as it will. Refuse to be average or to surrender to the chill of your spiritual environment.

A. W. Tozer

> Remember that "this, too, will pass." And remember that it will pass more quickly if you spend more time solving problems and less time fretting over them.

Hope looks for the good in people, opens doors for people, discovers what can be done to help, lights a candle, does not yield to cynicism. Hope sets people free.

Barbara Johnson

TRUST
GOD'S TIMETABLE

He has made everything appropriate in its time. He has also put eternity in their hearts, but man cannot discover the work God has done from beginning to end.

Ecclesiastes 3:11 HCSB

Are you anxious for God to work out His plan for your life? Who isn't? As believers, we all want God to do great things for us and through us, and we want Him to do those things now. But sometimes, God has other plans. Sometimes, God's timetable does not coincide with our own. It's worth noting, however, that God's timetable is always perfect.

The next time you find your patience tested to the limit, remember that the world unfolds according to God's plan, not ours. Sometimes, we must wait patiently, and that's as it should be. After all, think how patient God has been with us.

MORE FROM GOD'S WORD

Wait for the Lord; be courageous and let your heart be strong. Wait for the Lord.

Psalm 27:14 HCSB

He said to them, "It is not for you to know times or periods that the Father has set by His own authority."

Acts 1:7 HCSB

I wait for the LORD, my soul waits, and in his word I put my hope.

Psalm 130:5 NIV

I waited patiently for the LORD; and He inclined to me, and heard my cry.

Psalm 40:1 NKJV

SOME BIG IDEAS

Will not the Lord's time be better than your time?

C. H. Spurgeon

God has a designated time when his promise will be fulfilled and the prayer will be answered.

Jim Cymbala

When there is perplexity there is always guidance— not always at the moment we ask, but in good time, which is God's time. There is no need to fret and stew.

Elisabeth Elliot

Your times are in His hands. He's in charge of the timetable, so wait patiently.

Kay Arthur

God has very big plans in store for your life, so trust Him and wait patiently for those plans to unfold.

LET GOD GUIDE
THE WAY

The true children of God are those who let God's Spirit lead them.

Romans 8:14 NCV

The Bible promises that God will guide you if you let Him. Your job is to let Him. But sometimes, you will be tempted to do otherwise. Sometimes, you'll be tempted to go along with the crowd; other times, you'll be tempted to do things your way, not God's way. When you feel these temptations, resist them.

God has promised that when you ask for His help, He will not withhold it. So ask. Ask Him to meet the needs of your day. Ask Him to lead you, to protect you, and to correct you. And trust the answers He gives.

God stands at the door and waits. When you knock, He opens. When you ask, He answers. Your task, of course, is to seek His guidance prayerfully, confidently, and often.

MORE FROM GOD'S WORD

In all your ways acknowledge Him, and He shall direct your paths.

Proverbs 3:6 NKJV

Yet Lord, You are our Father; we are the clay, and You are our potter; we all are the work of Your hands.

Isaiah 64:8 HCSB

Lord, You are my lamp; the Lord illuminates my darkness.

2 Samuel 22:29 HCSB

Is God your spare wheel or your steering wheel? Make sure He's your steering wheel.

Lord, You light my lamp; my God illuminates my darkness.

Psalm 18:28 HCSB

OUT

SOME BIG IDEAS

We have ample evidence that the Lord is able to guide. The promises cover every imaginable situation. All we need to do is to take the hand he stretches out.

Elisabeth Elliot

Only He can guide you to invest your life in worthwhile ways. This guidance will come as you "walk" with Him and listen to Him.

Henry Blackaby and Claude King

Are you serious about wanting God's guidance to become a personal reality in your life? The first step is to tell God that you know you can't manage your own life; that you need his help.

Catherine Marshall

If we want to hear God's voice, we must surrender our minds and hearts to Him.

Billy Graham

GOD HAS A PLAN FOR YOU

You will show me the path of life.

Psalm 16:11 NKJV

You'll feel better about yourself if you're living on purpose, not by accident. But sometimes that's hard to do. Why? Because God's plans aren't always clear.

Sometimes we wander aimlessly in a wilderness of our own making. And sometimes, we struggle mightily against God in an unsuccessful attempt to find success and happiness through our own means, not His.

Are you genuinely trying to figure out God's purpose for your life? If so, you can be sure that with God's help, you will eventually discover it. So keep praying, and keep watching. And rest assured: God's got big plans for you . . . very big plans.

And when you discover those plans, you'll feel better about yourself . . . lots better.

MORE FROM GOD'S WORD

Who are those who fear the Lord? He will show them the path they should choose. They will live in prosperity, and their children will inherit the Promised Land.

Psalm 25:12-13 NLT

And we know that in all things God works for the good of those who love him, who have been called according to his purpose.

Romans 8:28 NIV

The steps of the Godly are directed by the Lord. He delights in every detail of their lives. Though they stumble, they will not fall, for the Lord holds them by the hand.

Psalm 37:23-24 NLT

It is God who works in you to will and to act according to his good purpose.

Philippians 2:13 NIV

NEXT

209

SOME BIG IDEAS

God is preparing you as his chosen arrow. As yet your shaft is hidden in his quiver, in the shadows, but, at the precise moment, he will reach for you and launch you to that place of his appointment.

Charles Swindoll

When the dream of our heart is one that God has planted there, a strange happiness flows into us. At that moment, all of the spiritual resources of the universe are released to help us. Our praying is then at one with the will of God and becomes a channel for the Creator's purposes for us and our world.

Catherine Marshall

God has very big plans in store for your life, so trust Him and wait patiently for those plans to unfold. And remember: God's timing is best.

With God, it's never "Plan B" or "second best." It's always "Plan A." And, if we let Him, He'll make something beautiful of our lives.

Gloria Gaither

NOTHING IS IMPOSSIBLE FOR GOD

Is anything too hard for the LORD?

Genesis 18:14 KJV

If you haven't seen any of God's miracles lately, you haven't been looking. Throughout history, the Creator has intervened in the course of human events in ways that cannot be explained by science or human rationale. And He's still doing so today.

God's miracles are not limited to special occasions, nor are they witnessed by a select few. God is crafting His wonders all around us: the miracle of the birth of a new baby; the miracle of a world renewing itself with every sunrise; the miracle of lives transformed by God's love and grace. Each day, God's handiwork is evident for all to see and experience.

Today, seize the opportunity to inspect God's hand at work. His miracles come in a variety of shapes and sizes, so keep your eyes and your heart open. Be watchful, and you'll soon be amazed.

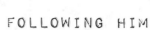
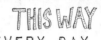

MORE FROM GOD'S WORD

For the Lord your God is the God of gods and Lord of lords, the great, mighty, and awesome God.

Deuteronomy 10:17 HCSB

But Jesus looked at them and said, "With men this is impossible, but with God all things are possible."

Matthew 19:26 HCSB

You are the God who works wonders; You revealed Your strength among the peoples.

Psalm 77:14 HCSB

Ah, Lord God! Behold, You have made the heavens and the earth by Your great power and outstretched arm. There is nothing too hard for You.

Jeremiah 32:17 NKJV

SOME BIG IDEAS

If we take God's program, we can have God's power—not otherwise.

E. Stanley Jones

You can believe in the Holy Spirit not because you see Him, but because you see what He does in people's lives when they are surrendered to Christ and possess His power.

Billy Graham

No giant will ever be a match for a big God with a little rock.

Beth Moore

Today, as a way of managing stress, think of all the wonderful things that God has done for you. And then, take time to ponder His promises for the future. When you focus on God's gifts, you won't stay stressed for long.

The task ahead of us is never as great as the Power behind us.

Anonymous

BE HUMBLE

Therefore humble yourselves under the mighty hand of God, that He may exalt you in due time.

1 Peter 5:6 NKJV

On the road to spiritual growth, pride is a massive roadblock. The more prideful you are, the more difficult it is to know God. When you experience success, it's easy to puff out your chest and proclaim, "I did that!" But it's wrong. Dietrich Bonhoeffer was correct when he observed, "It is very easy to overestimate the importance of our own achievements in comparison with what we owe others." In other words, reality breeds humility. So if you want to know God better, be humble. Otherwise, you'll be building a roadblock between you and your Creator (and that's a very bad thing to do!).

MORE FROM GOD'S WORD

If My people who are called by My name will humble themselves, and pray and seek My face, and turn from their wicked ways, then I will hear from heaven, and will forgive their sin and heal their land.

2 Chronicles 7:14 NKJV

Do nothing out of rivalry or conceit, but in humility consider others as more important than yourselves.

Philippians 2:3 HCSB

Let another praise you, and not your own mouth—a stranger, and not your own lips.

Proverbs 27:2 HCSB

But He said to me, "My grace is sufficient for you, for power is perfected in weakness." Therefore, I will most gladly boast all the more about my weaknesses, so that Christ's power may reside in me.

2 Corinthians 12:9 HCSB

215

 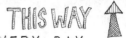

SOME BIG IDEAS

Do you wish to rise? Begin by descending. You plan a tower that will pierce the clouds? Lay first the foundation of humility.

St. Augustine

The great characteristic of the saint is humility.

Oswald Chambers

Do you value humility above status? If so, God will smile upon your endeavors. But if you value status above humility, you're inviting God's displeasure. In short, humility pleases God; pride does not.

Nothing sets a person so much out of the devil's reach as humility.

Jonathan Edwards

We are never stronger than the moment we admit we are weak.

Beth Moore

AVOID GOSSIP

So rid yourselves of all wickedness, all deceit, hypocrisy, envy, and all slander.

1 Peter 2:1 HCSB

Face facts: gossip is the guilty little pleasure that tempts almost all of us from time to time. Why is it so tempting to gossip? Because when we put other people down, we experience a brief dose of self-righteousness as we look down our noses at the misdeeds of others. But there's a catch: in truth, we can never really build ourselves up by tearing other people down. So the habit of gossip turns out to be a self-defeating waste of time.

It's no wonder that the Bible clearly teaches that gossip is wrong. Consider the simple advice found in Proverbs 16:28: "Gossip ruins friendships" (NCV). So do yourself a big favor: don't spend precious time talking about other people. It's a waste of words, it's the wrong thing to do, and in the end, it will leave you with less self-respect, not more.

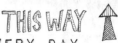
When you avoid the temptation to engage in gossip, you'll feel better about yourself—and other people will feel better about you, too. So don't do it.

MORE FROM GOD'S WORD

Seek to lead a quiet life, to mind your own business, and to work with your own hands, as we commanded you.

1 Thessalonians 4:11 HCSB

But now you must also put away all the following: anger, wrath, malice, slander, and filthy language from your mouth.

Colossians 3:8 HCSB

There is nothing covered that won't be uncovered; nothing hidden that won't be made known. Therefore whatever you have said in the dark will be heard in the light, and what you have whispered in an ear in private rooms will be proclaimed on the housetops.

Luke 12:2-3 HCSB

GOSSIP CAN HURT

Has anyone ever spread a rumor or gossip about you or one of your friends? Spend a few minutes writing how that made you feel and why it is a bad thing to do to others.

_____

_____

_____

_____

_____

_____

_____

_____

_____

_____

_____

_____

SOME BIG IDEAS

Change the heart, and you change the speech.

Warren Wiersbe

The great test of a man's character is his tongue.

Oswald Chambers

To belittle is to be little.

Anonymous

The cost of gossip always exceeds its worth.

Marie T. Freeman

When talking about other people, use this guideline: don't say something behind someone's back that you wouldn't say to that person directly.

THE RIGHT KIND OF HABITS

I, the Lord, examine the mind, I test the heart to give to each according to his way, according to what his actions deserve.

Jeremiah 17:10 HCSB

It's an old saying and a true one: First, you make your habits, and then your habits make you. Some habits will inevitably bring you closer to God; other habits will lead you away from the path He has chosen for you. If you sincerely desire to improve your spiritual health, you must honestly examine the habits that make up the fabric of your day. And you must abandon those habits that are displeasing to God.

If you trust God, and if you keep asking for His help, He can transform your life. If you sincerely ask Him to help you, the same God who created the universe will help you defeat the harmful habits that have so far defeated you. If at first you don't succeed, keep praying. God is listening, and He's ready to help you become a better person if you ask Him . . . so ask today.

MORE FROM GOD'S WORD

Dear friend, I pray that you may prosper in every way and be in good health, just as your soul prospers.

3 John 1:2 HCSB

Therefore, brothers, by the mercies of God, I urge you to present your bodies as a living sacrifice, holy and pleasing to God; this is your spiritual worship.

Romans 12:1 HCSB

Don't you know that you are God's sanctuary and that the Spirit of God lives in you?

1 Corinthians 3:16 HCSB

Do you not know that your body is a sanctuary of the Holy Spirit who is in you, whom you have from God? You are not your own, for you were bought at a price; therefore glorify God in your body.

1 Corinthians 6:19-20 HCSB

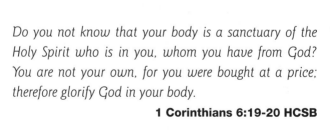

ENTER
EXIT

100 ESSENTIAL DEVOS FOR TWEENS

YOUR HABITS

List some of your good habits.

_____

_____

_____

_____

_____

List some of your bad habits.

_____

_____

_____

_____

_____

_____

Now find some ways to better the good habits
and defeat the bad. Pray on it.

223

SOME BIG IDEAS

You can build up a set of good habits so that you habitually take the Christian way without thought.

E. Stanley Jones

First you make your habits; then your habits make you. So it's always a good time to think about the kind of person your habits are making you.

You will never change your life until you change something you do daily.

John Maxwell

If you want to form a new habit, get to work. If you want to break a bad habit, get on your knees.

Marie T. Freeman

Since behaviors become habits, make them work with you and not against you.

E. Stanley Jones

HOLINESS BEFORE HAPPINESS

Blessed are those who hunger and thirst for righteousness, because they will be filled.

Matthew 5:6 HCSB

Because you are an imperfect human being, you are not "perfectly" happy—and that's perfectly okay with God. He is far less concerned with your happiness than He is with your holiness.

God continuously reveals Himself in everyday life, but He does not do so in order to make you contented; He does so in order to lead you to His Son. So don't be overly concerned with your current level of happiness; it will change. Be more concerned with the current state of your relationship with Christ: He does not change. And because your Savior transcends time and space, you can be comforted in the knowledge that in the end, His joy will become your joy . . . for all eternity.

THIS WAY

FOLLOWING HIM EVERY DAY

MORE FROM GOD'S WORD

Real wisdom, God's wisdom, begins with a holy life and is characterized by getting along with others. It is gentle and reasonable, overflowing with mercy and blessings, not hot one day and cold the next, not two-faced.

James 3:17 MSG

Pursue peace with all people, and holiness, without which no one will see the Lord:

Hebrews 12:14 NKJV

Since everything here today might well be gone tomorrow, do you see how essential it is to live a holy life?

2 Peter 3:11 MSG

But now you must be holy in everything you do, just as God—who chose you to be his children—is holy. For he himself has said, "You must be holy because I am holy."

1 Peter 1:15-16 NLT

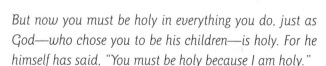

SOME BIG IDEAS

You don't have to be like the world to have an impact on the world. You don't have to be like the crowd to change the crowd. You don't have to lower yourself down to their level to lift them up to your level. Holiness doesn't seek to be odd. Holiness seeks to be like God.

Max Lucado

A holy life simply is a life that works.

Richard Foster

Holiness isn't in a style of dress. It's not a matter of rules and regulations. It's a way of life that emanates quietness and rest, joy in family, shared pleasures with friends, the help of a neighbor—and the hope of a Savior.

Joni Eareckson Tada

Sin will grow without sowing, but holiness needs cultivation.
C. H. Spurgeon

227

BE CAREFUL
HOW YOU DIRECT
YOUR THOUGHTS

Finally brothers, whatever is true, whatever is honorable, whatever is just, whatever is pure, whatever is lovely, whatever is commendable—if there is any moral excellence and if there is any praise—dwell on these things.

Philippians 4:8 HCSB

How will you direct your thoughts today? Will you obey the words of Philippians 4:8 by dwelling upon those things that are honorable, true, and worthy of praise? Or will you allow your thoughts to be hijacked by the negativity that seems to dominate our troubled world?

Are you fearful, angry, bored, or worried? Are you so preoccupied with the concerns of this day that you fail to thank God for the promise of eternity? Are you confused, bitter, or pessimistic? If so, God wants to have a little talk with you. He wants to remind you of His infinite love and His boundless grace. As you contemplate these things, and as you give thanks for God's blessings, negativity should no longer dominate your day or your life.

MORE FROM GOD'S WORD

So prepare your minds for service and have self-control.

1 Peter 1:13 NCV

Those who are pure in their thinking are happy, because they will be with God.

Matthew 5:8 NCV

Commit your works to the Lord, and your thoughts will be established.

Proverbs 16:3 NKJV

Brothers, don't be childish in your thinking, but be infants in evil and adult in your thinking.

1 Corinthians 14:20 HCSB

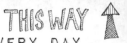

SOME BIG IDEAS

Our own possible bad thoughts and deeds are far more dangerous to us than any enemy from the world.

St. Ambrose

We know well enough how to keep outward silence, and to hush our spoken words, but we know little of interior silence. It consists in hushing our idle, restless, wandering imagination, in quieting the promptings of our worldly minds, and in suppressing the crowd of unprofitable thoughts which excite and disturb the soul.

François Fènelon

Good thoughts can lead you to some very good places . . . and bad thoughts can lead elsewhere. So guard your thoughts accordingly.

People who do not develop and practice good thinking often find themselves at the mercy of their circumstances.

John Maxwell

I became aware of one very important concept I had missed before: my attitude—not my circumstances—was what was making me unhappy.

Vonette Bright

GOD IS
TRUSTWORTHY

It is better to trust the Lord than to put confidence in people. It is better to trust the Lord than to put confidence in princes.

Psalm 118:8-9 NLT

Sometimes the future seems bright, and sometimes it does not. Yet even when we cannot see the possibilities of tomorrow, God can. As believers, our challenge is to trust an uncertain future to an all-powerful God.

When we trust God, we should trust Him without reservation. We should steel ourselves against the inevitable stresses of the day, secure in the knowledge that our Heavenly Father has a plan for the future that only He can see.

Can you place your future into the hands of a loving and all-knowing God? Can you live amid the uncertainties of today, knowing that God has dominion over all your tomorrows? If you can, you are wise and you

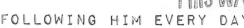

are blessed. When you trust God with everything you are and everything you have, He will bless you now and forever.

MORE FROM GOD'S WORD

Trust in the Lord with all your heart, and do not rely on your own understanding; think about Him in all your ways, and He will guide you on the right paths.

Proverbs 3:5-6 HCSB

For the eyes of the Lord range throughout the earth to show Himself strong for those whose hearts are completely His.

2 Chronicles 16:9 HCSB

He granted their request because they trusted in Him.

1 Chronicles 5:20 HCSB

Let us hold fast the confession of our hope without wavering, for He who promised is faithful.

Hebrews 10:23 NKJV

OUT

SOME BIG IDEAS

Conditions are always changing; therefore, I must not be dependent upon conditions. What matters supremely is my soul and my relationship to God.

Corrie ten Boom

True faith is man's weakness leaning on God's strength.

D. L. Moody

Sometimes the very essence of faith is trusting God in the midst of things He knows good and well we cannot comprehend.

Beth Moore

Are you serious about wanting God's guidance to become the person he wants you to be? The first step is to tell God that you know you can't manage your own life; that you need his help.

Catherine Marshall

> One of the most important lessons that you can ever learn is to trust God for every-thing—not some things, not most things . . . every-thing!

DURING
DIFFICULT DAYS

God is our refuge and strength, a helper who is always found in times of trouble.

Psalm 46:1 HCSB

All of us face difficult days. Sometimes even the most devout Christians can become discouraged, and you are no exception. After all, you live in a world where expectations can be high and demands can be even higher.

If you find yourself enduring difficult circumstances, remember that God remains in His heaven. If you become discouraged with the direction of your day or your life, turn your thoughts and prayers to Him. He is a God of possibility, not negativity. He will guide you through your difficulties and beyond them. And then, with a renewed spirit of optimism and hope, you can thank the Giver of all things good for gifts that are simply too numerous to count.

MORE FROM GOD'S WORD

We also have joy with our troubles, because we know that these troubles produce patience. And patience produces character, and character produces hope.

Romans 5:3-4 NCV

The LORD also will be a stronghold for the oppressed, a stronghold in times of trouble.

Psalm 9:9 NASB

Come to Me, all you who labor and are heavy laden, and I will give you rest. Take My yoke upon you and learn from Me, for I am gentle and lowly in heart, and you will find rest for your souls. For My yoke is easy and My burden is light.

Matthew 11:28-30 NKJV

I called to the Lord in my distress; I called to my God. From His temple He heard my voice.

2 Samuel 22:7 HCSB

NEXT

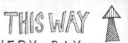

SOME BIG IDEAS

Even in the winter, even in the midst of the storm, the sun is still there. Somewhere, up above the clouds, it still shines and warms and pulls at the life buried deep inside the brown branches and frozen earth. The sun is there! Spring will come.

Gloria Gaither

The strengthening of faith comes from staying with it in the hour of trial. We should not shrink from tests of faith.

Catherine Marshall

Our heavenly Father never takes anything from his children unless he means to give them something better.

George Mueller

In dealing with difficult situations, view God as your comfort and your strength. And remember: Tough times can also be times of intense personal growth.

ENTRUSTING YOUR HOPES TO GOD

You, Lord, give true peace to those who depend on you, because they trust you.

Isaiah 26:3 NCV

There are few sadder sights on earth than the sight of a girl or guy who has lost hope. In difficult times, hope can be elusive, but those who place their faith in God's promises need never lose it. After all, God is good; His love endures; He has promised His children the gift of eternal life. And, God keeps His promises.

If you find yourself falling into the spiritual traps of worry and discouragement, seek the healing touch of Jesus and the encouraging words of fellow believers. And if you find a friend in need, remind him or her of the peace that is found through a genuine relationship with Christ. It was Christ who promised, "I have told you these things so that in Me you may have peace. In the world you have suffering. But take courage! I have

ENTER
EXIT

conquered the world" (John 16:33 HCSB). This world can be a place of trials and troubles, but as believers, we are secure. God has promised us peace, joy, and eternal life. And, of course, God keeps His promises today, tomorrow, and forever.

MORE FROM GOD'S WORD

But if we hope for what we do not see, we eagerly wait for it with patience.

Romans 8:25 HCSB

Now may the God of hope fill you with all joy and peace in believing, so that you may overflow with hope by the power of the Holy Spirit.

Romans 15:13 HCSB

Be of good courage, and he shall strengthen your heart, all ye that hope in the LORD.

Psalm 31:24 KJV

Be joyful in hope, patient in affliction, faithful in prayer.

Romans 12:12 NIV

YOUR HOPES AND DREAMS

Take a few minutes to think about your hopes,
your dreams, and your worries. Then jot them
down below. Don't forget to pray to God about
these things. He can help.

_____

_____

_____

_____

_____

_____

_____

_____

_____

_____

_____

_____

_____

SOME BIG IDEAS

Hope is faith holding out its hand in the dark.

Barbara Johnson

The will of God is the most delicious and delightful thing in the universe.

Hannah Whitall Smith

It is more serious to lose hope than to sin.

John of Carpathos

God's purposes are often hidden from us. He owes us no explanations. We owe Him our complete love and trust.

Warren Wiersbe

The resurrection of Jesus, the whole alphabet of human hope, the certificate of our Lord's mission from heaven, is the heart of the gospel in all ages.

R. G. Lee

DEVO 76

IT'S A WONDERFUL LIFE

I came so they can have real and eternal life, more and better life than they ever dreamed of.

John 10:10 MSG

Life can be tough sometimes, but it's also wonderful—and it's a glorious gift from God. How will you use that gift? Every day, including this one, comes gift-wrapped from God—your job is to unwrap that gift, to use it wisely, and to give thanks to the Giver.

Instead of sleepwalking through life, you must wake up and live in the precious present. Each waking moment holds the potential to celebrate, to serve, to share, or to love. Because you are a person with incalculable potential, each moment has incalculable value. Your challenge is to experience each day to the fullest as you seek to live in accordance with God's plan for your life. When you do, you'll experience His abundance and His peace.

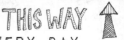

Are you willing to treat this day (and every one hereafter) as a special gift to be savored and celebrated? You should—and if you seek to Live with a capital L, you most certainly will.

MORE FROM GOD'S WORD

Make it your ambition to lead a quiet life, to mind your own business and to work with your hands, just as we told you, so that your daily life may win the respect of outsiders and so that you will not be dependent on anybody.

1 Thessalonians 4:11-12 NIV

I urge you to live a life worthy of the calling you have received.

Ephesians 4:1 NIV

I am the way and the truth and the life. No one comes to the Father except through me.

John 14:6 NIV

SOME BIG IDEAS

Life is a glorious opportunity.

Billy Graham

People, places, and things were never meant to give us life. God alone is the author of a fulfilling life.

Gary Smalley & John Trent

The Christian life is motivated, not by a list of do's and don'ts, but by the gracious outpouring of God's love and blessing.

Anne Graham Lotz

I beg you do not squander life. And don't live for this world only.

Billy Graham

Life is a priceless gift from God. Spend time each day thanking God for His gift.

LISTEN TO GOD

The one who is from God listens to God's words. This is why you don't listen, because you are not from God.

John 8:47 HCSB

Sometimes God speaks loudly and clearly. More often, He speaks in a quiet voice—and if you are wise, you will be listening carefully when He does. To do so, you must carve out quiet moments each day to study His Word and sense His direction.

Can you quiet yourself long enough to listen to your conscience? Are you attuned to the subtle guidance of your intuition? Are you willing to pray sincerely and then to wait quietly for God's response? Hopefully so. Usually God refrains from sending His messages on stone tablets or city billboards. More often, He communicates in subtler ways. If you sincerely desire to hear His voice, you must listen carefully, and you must do so in the silent corners of your quiet, willing heart.

Listen in silence before me . . . .

Isaiah 41:1 NLT

God has no use for the prayers of the people who won't listen to him.

Proverbs 28:9 MSG

Trust God from the bottom of your heart; don't try to figure out everything on your own. Listen for God's voice in everything you do, everywhere you go; he's the one who will keep you on track.

Proverbs 3:5-6 MSG

You must follow the Lord your God and fear Him. You must keep His commands and listen to His voice; you must worship Him and remain faithful to Him.

Deuteronomy 13:4 HCSB

NEXT

SOME BIG IDEAS

When we come to Jesus stripped of pretensions, with a needy spirit, ready to listen, He meets us at the point of need.

Catherine Marshall

God is always listening.

Stormie Omartian

Listening is loving.

Zig Ziglar

Prayer is two-way communication with God. Talking to God isn't enough; you should also listen to Him.

In the soul-searching of our lives, we are to stay quiet so we can hear Him say all that He wants to say to us in our hearts.

Charles Swindoll

LOOK

DON'T OVERESTIMATE THE IMPORTANCE OF STUFF

And He told them, "Watch out and be on guard against all greed, because one's life is not in the abundance of his possessions."

Luke 12:15 HCSB

How important are our material possessions? Not as important as we might think. In a well-balanced life, material possessions should play a rather small role. Of course, we all need the basic necessities of life, but once we meet those needs for ourselves and for our families, the piling up of possessions often creates more problems than it solves. Our real riches are not of this world. We are never really rich until we are rich in spirit.

If you've become preoccupied with money and the things that money can buy, it's time to de-emphasize things material and re-emphasize things spiritual. When you do, you'll feel better about yourself . . . and

FOLLOW

ENTER
EXIT

you'll begin storing up riches that will endure forever: the spiritual kind.

MORE FROM GOD'S WORD

He who trusts in his riches will fall, but the righteous will flourish . . . .

Proverbs 11:28 NKJV

No one can serve two masters. The person will hate one master and love the other, or will follow one master and refuse to follow the other. You cannot serve both God and worldly riches.

Matthew 6:24 NCV

For the mind-set of the flesh is death, but the mind-set of the Spirit is life and peace.

Romans 8:6 HCSB

Since we entered the world penniless and will leave it penniless, if we have bread on the table and shoes on our feet, that's enough.

1 Timothy 6:7-8 MSG

SOME BIG IDEAS

A society that pursues pleasure runs the risk of raising expectations ever higher, so that true contentment always lies tantalizingly out of reach.

Philip Yancey and Paul Brand

It's sobering to contemplate how much time, effort, sacrifice, compromise, and attention we give to acquiring and increasing our supply of something that is totally insignificant in eternity.

Anne Graham Lotz

The more we stuff ourselves with material pleasures, the less we seem to appreciate life.

Barbara Johnson

When possessions become our god, we become materialistic and greedy . . . and we forfeit our contentment and our joy.

Charles Swindoll

> Too much stuff doesn't ensure happiness nor does it build lasting self-esteem. In fact, having too much stuff can actually prevent happiness.

REMEMBER THAT ACTIONS SPEAK LOUDER

For the kingdom of God is not in talk but in power.

1 Corinthians 4:20 HCSB

The old saying is both familiar and true: actions speak louder than words. And as believers, we must beware: our actions should always give credence to the changes that Christ can make in the lives of those who walk with Him.

God calls upon each of us to act in accordance with His will and with respect for His commandments. If we are to be responsible believers, we must realize that it is never enough simply to hear the instructions of God; we must also live by them. And it is never enough to wait idly by while others do God's work here on earth; we, too, must act. Doing God's work is a responsibility that each of us must bear, and when we do, our loving Heavenly Father rewards our efforts with a bountiful harvest.

MORE FROM GOD'S WORD

Therefore, get your minds ready for action, being self-disciplined, and set your hope completely on the grace to be brought to you at the revelation of Jesus Christ.

1 Peter 1:13 HCSB

But prove yourselves doers of the word, and not merely hearers.

James 1:22 NASB

Are there those among you who are truly wise and understanding? Then they should show it by living right and doing good things with a gentleness that comes from wisdom.

James 3:13 NCV

The prudent see danger and take refuge, but the simple keep going and suffer from it.

Proverbs 27:12 NIV

NEXT

SOME BIG IDEAS

Every word we speak, every action we take, has an effect on the totality of humanity. No one can escape that privilege—or that responsibility.

Laurie Beth Jones

It is by acts and not by ideas that people live.

Harry Emerson Fosdick

Try as we might, we simply cannot escape the consequences of our actions. How we behave today has a direct impact on the rewards we will receive tomorrow.

Never fail to do something because you don't feel like it. Sometimes you just have to do it now, and you'll feel like it later.

Marie T. Freeman

Do noble things, do not dream them all day long.

Charles Kingsley

MAKE CHRIST YOUR FOCUS

Then Jesus spoke to them again: "I am the light of the world. Anyone who follows Me will never walk in the darkness, but will have the light of life."

John 8:12 HCSB

Is Christ the focus of your life? Are you fired with enthusiasm for Him? Are you an energized Christian who allows God's Son to reign over every aspect of your day? Make no mistake: that's exactly what God intends for you to do.

God has given you the gift of eternal life through His Son. In response to God's priceless gift, you are instructed to focus your thoughts, your prayers, and your energies upon God and His only begotten Son. To do so, you must resist the subtle yet powerful temptation to become a "spiritual dabbler."

A person who dabbles in the Christian faith is unwilling to place God in His rightful place: above all other things. Resist that temptation; make God the

FOLLOWING HIM EVERY DAY

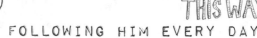

cornerstone and the touchstone of your life. When you do, He will give you all the strength and wisdom you need to live victoriously for Him.

MORE FROM GOD'S WORD

Then He said to them all, "If anyone wants to come with Me, he must deny himself, take up his cross daily, and follow Me."

Luke 9:23 HCSB

Love consists in this: not that we loved God, but that He loved us and sent His Son to be the propitiation for our sins.

1 John 4:10 HCSB

Therefore if any man be in Christ, he is a new creature: old things are passed away; behold, all things are become new.

2 Corinthians 5:17 KJV

Jesus Christ is the same yesterday, today, and forever.

Hebrews 13:8 HCSB

OUT

SOME BIG IDEAS

I am truly happy with Jesus Christ. I couldn't live without Him. When my life gets beyond the ability to cope, He takes over.

Ruth Bell Graham

Whatever is your best time in the day, give that to communion with God.

Hudson Taylor

Give me the person who says, "This one thing I do, and not these fifty things I dabble in."

D. L. Moody

I don't see how any Christian can survive, let alone live life as more than a conqueror, apart from a quiet time alone with God.

Kay Arthur

> Jesus is the light of the world. God wants Him to be the light of your life.

255

DON'T BE JUDGMENTAL

Stop judging others, and you will not be judged. Stop criticizing others, or it will all come back on you. If you forgive others, you will be forgiven.

Luke 6:37 NLT

Here's something worth thinking about: If you judge other people harshly, God will judge you in the same fashion. But that's not all (thank goodness!). The Bible also promises that if you forgive others, you, too, will be forgiven. Have you developed the bad habit of behaving yourself like an amateur judge and jury, assigning blame and condemnation wherever you go? If so, it's time to grow up and obey God. When it comes to judging everything and everybody, God doesn't need your help . . . and He doesn't want it.

MORE FROM GOD'S WORD

Why do you look at the speck in your brother's eye, but don't notice the log in your own eye? Or how can you say to your brother, "Let me take the speck out of your eye," and look, there's a log in your eye? Hypocrite! First take the log out of your eye, and then you will see clearly to take the speck out of your brother's eye.

Matthew 7:3-5 HCSB

You, therefore, have no excuse, you who pass judgment on someone else, for at whatever point you judge the other, you are condemning yourself.

Romans 2:1 NIV

So when they continued asking him, he lifted up himself, and said unto them, He that is without sin among you, let him first cast a stone at her.

John 8:7 KJV

Speak and act as those who will be judged by the law of freedom. For judgment is without mercy to the one who hasn't shown mercy. Mercy triumphs over judgment.

James 2:12-13 HCSB

NEXT

SOME BIG IDEAS

Christians think they are prosecuting attorneys or judges, when, in reality, God has called all of us to be witnesses.

Warren Wiersbe

It is time that the followers of Jesus revise their language and learn to speak respectfully of non-Christian peoples.

Lottie Moon

Your ability to judge others requires a divine insight that you simply don't have. So do everybody (including yourself) a favor: don't judge.

Jesus lives in the community; He only visits the church.

Anonymous

Judging draws the judgment of others.

Catherine Marshall

BE KIND TO EVERYBODY

And be kind and compassionate to one another, forgiving one another, just as God also forgave you in Christ.

Ephesians 4:32 HCSB

Would you like an ironclad formula for improved self-esteem? Try this: be kind to everybody.

Kindness is a choice. Sometimes, when you feel happy or generous, you may find it easy to be kind. Other times, when you are discouraged or tired, you can scarcely summon the energy to utter a single kind word. But, God's commandment is clear: He intends that you make the conscious choice to treat others with kindness and respect, no matter your circumstances, no matter your emotions.

So today, spread a heaping helping of kindness wherever you go. When you do, you'll discover that the more kindness you give away to others, the more you'll receive in return.

MORE FROM GOD'S WORD

Finally, all of you be of one mind, having compassion for one another; love as brothers, be tenderhearted, be courteous.

1 Peter 3:8 NKJV

Love is patient; love is kind.

1 Corinthians 13:4 HCSB

And may the Lord make you increase and abound in love to one another and to all.

1 Thessalonians 3:12 NKJV

Pure and undefiled religion before our God and Father is this: to look after orphans and widows in their distress and to keep oneself unstained by the world.

James 1:27 HCSB

KINDNESS AT WORK

Sometime within the next week go out of your way (more than once) to be kind to someone . . . without seeking a reward. In the boxes below, write or draw about what you did and how it made you feel.

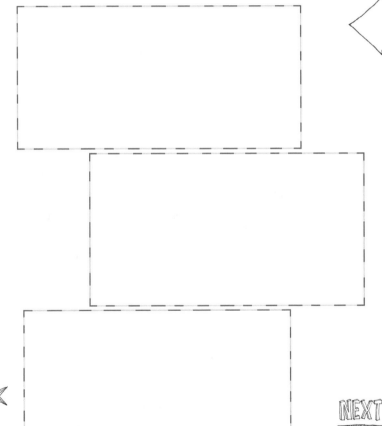

SOME BIG IDEAS

A little kindly advice is better than a great deal of scolding.

Fanny Crosby

When you launch an act of kindness out into the crosswinds of life, it will blow kindness back to you.

Dennis Swanberg

When in doubt, be a little kinder than necessary. You'll feel better about yourself when you do.

When you extend hospitality to others, you're not trying to impress people, you're trying to reflect God to them.

Max Lucado

Do all the good you can. By all the means you can. In all the ways you can. In all the places you can. At all the times you can. To all the people you can. As long as ever you can.

John Wesley

DEVO 83

KEEP LEARNING
EVERY DAY

It takes knowledge to fill a home with rare and beautiful treasures.

Proverbs 24:4 NCV

Another way to feel better about yourself is to keep acquiring both knowledge and wisdom. Knowledge is found in textbooks. Wisdom, on the other hand, is found in God's Holy Word and in the carefully-chosen words of loving parents, family members, and friends.

Knowledge is an important building block in a well-lived life, and it pays rich dividends both personally and professionally. But, wisdom is even more important because it refashions not only the mind, but also the heart.

When you study God's Word and live according to His commandments, you will become wise . . . and you will be a blessing to your family and to the world.

ENTER
EXIT

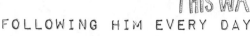
MORE FROM GOD'S WORD

A wise person pays attention to correction that will improve his life.

Proverbs 15:31 ICB

Remember what you are taught, and listen carefully to words of knowledge.

Proverbs 23:12 NCV

The fear of the Lord is the beginning of knowledge, but fools despise wisdom and discipline.

Proverbs 1:7 NIV

The knowledge of the secrets of the kingdom of heaven has been given to you . . . .

Matthew 13:11 NIV

OUT

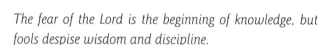

SOME BIG IDEAS

While chastening is always difficult, if we look to God for the lesson we should learn, we will see spiritual fruit.

Vonette Bright

The wonderful thing about God's schoolroom is that we get to grade our own papers. You see, He doesn't test us so He can learn how well we're doing. He tests us so we can discover how well we're doing.

Charles Swindoll

The wise man gives proper appreciation in his life to his past. He learns to sift the sawdust of heritage in order to find the nuggets that make the current moment have any meaning.

Grady Nutt

> Keep learning. The future belongs to those who are willing to do the work that's required to prepare for it.

It's the things you learn after you know it all that really count.

Vance Havner

MAKE THE MOST OF YOUR TALENTS

Do not neglect the gift that is in you.

1 Timothy 4:14 HCSB

Face it: you've got an array of talents that need to be refined—and you'll feel better about yourself when you refine them. But nobody will force you to do the hard work of converting raw talent into prime-time talent. That's a job you must do for yourself.

Today, make a promise to yourself that you will earnestly seek to discover the talents that God has given you. Then, nourish those talents and make them grow. Finally, vow to share your gifts with the world for as long as God gives you the power to do so. When you do, you'll feel better about yourself and your abilities . . . and the world will, too.

MORE FROM GOD'S WORD

God has given gifts to each of you from his great variety of spiritual gifts. Manage them well so that God's generosity can flow through you.

1 Peter 4:10 NLT

Now there are varieties of gifts, but the same Spirit. And there are varieties of ministries, and the same Lord.

1 Corinthians 12:4-5 NASB

The man who had received the five talents brought the other five. "Master," he said, "you entrusted me with five talents. See, I have gained five more." His master replied, "Well done, good and faithful servant! You have been faithful with a few things; I will put you in charge of many things. Come and share your master's happiness."

Matthew 25:20-21 NIV

Whatever you do, do it enthusiastically, as something done for the Lord and not for men.

Colossians 3:23 HCSB

SOME BIG IDEAS

Employ whatever God has entrusted you with, in doing good, all possible good, in every possible kind and degree.

John Wesley

God often reveals His direction for our lives through the way He made us . . . with a certain personality and unique skills.

Bill Hybels

You have special abilities that can be nurtured carefully or ignored totally. The challenge, of course, is to do the former and to avoid the latter.

If you want to reach your potential, you need to add a strong work ethic to your talent.

John Maxwell

You are the only person on earth who can use your ability.

Zig Ziglar

DEVO 85

SPEND TIME WITH GOD EVERY MORNING

Morning by morning he wakens me and opens my understanding to his will. The Sovereign Lord has spoken to me, and I have listened.

Isaiah 50:4-5 NLT

Want to strengthen your faith? Then schedule a meeting with God every day.

Daily life is a tapestry of habits, and no habit is more important to your spiritual health than the discipline of daily prayer and devotion to the Creator. When you begin each day with your head bowed and your heart lifted, you are reminded of God's love and God's laws.

When you do engage in a regular regimen of worship and praise, God will reward you for your wisdom and your obedience. Each new day is a gift from God, and if you're wise, you'll spend a few quiet moments thanking the Giver. It's a wonderful way to start your day.

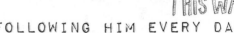
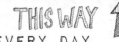
MORE FROM GOD'S WORD

It is good to give thanks to the Lord, to sing praises to the Most High. It is good to proclaim your unfailing love in the morning, your faithfulness in the evening.

Psalm 92:1-2 NLT

Make an appointment with God and keep it. Bible study and prayer should be at the top of your to-do list, not the bottom.

But grow in the grace and knowledge of our Lord and Savior Jesus Christ. To Him be the glory both now and to the day of eternity.

2 Peter 3:18 HCSB

Teach me Your way, Lord, and I will live by Your truth. Give me an undivided mind to fear Your name.

Psalm 86:11 HCSB

In all your ways acknowledge Him, and He shall direct your paths.

Proverbs 3:6 NKJV

SOME BIG IDEAS

The moment you wake up each morning, all your wishes and hopes for the day rush at you like wild animals. And the first job each morning consists in shoving it all back; in listening to that other voice, taking that other point of view, letting that other, larger, stronger, quieter life coming flowing in.

C. S. Lewis

A person with no devotional life generally struggles with faith and obedience.

Charles Stanley

Mark it down. God never turns away the honest seeker. Go to God with your questions. You may not find all the answers, but in finding God, you know the One who does.

Max Lucado

Maintenance of the devotional mood is indispensable to success in the Christian life.

A. W. Tozer

YOU SHOULD NEVER BE TOO BUSY FOR GOD

Don't burn out; keep yourselves fueled and aflame. Be alert servants of the Master, cheerfully expectant. Don't quit in hard times; pray all the harder.

Romans 12:11-12 MSG

Each day has 1,440 minutes—do you value your relationship with God enough to spend a few of those minutes with Him? He deserves that much of your time and more. But if you find that you're simply "too busy" for a daily chat with your Father in heaven, it's time to take a long, hard look at your priorities and your values.

If you've acquired the unfortunate habit of trying to "squeeze" God into the corners of your life, it's time to reshuffle the items on your to-do list by placing God first. He wants your undivided attention, not the leftovers of your day. So, if you haven't already done so, form the habit of spending quality time with God. He deserves it . . . and so, for that matter, do you.

MORE FROM GOD'S WORD

Careful planning puts you ahead in the long run; hurry and scurry puts you further behind.

Proverbs 21:5 MSG

You can't go wrong when you love others. When you add up everything in the law code, the sum total is love. But make sure that you don't get so absorbed and exhausted in taking care of all your day-by-day obligations that you lose track of the time and doze off, oblivious to God.

Romans 13:10-11 MSG

Jesus said, "You're tied down to the mundane; I'm in touch with what is beyond your horizons. You live in terms of what you see and touch. I'm living on other terms. I told you that you were missing God in all this. You're at a dead end. If you won't believe I am who I say I am, you're at the dead end of sins. You're missing God in your lives."

John 8:23-24 MSG

Be careful not to forget the Lord.

Deuteronomy 6:12 HCSB

SOME BIG IDEAS

To be successful, you can't just run on the fast track: run on your track.

John Maxwell

Often our lives are strangled by things that don't ultimately matter.

Grady Nutt

The prayer of the feeblest saint who lives in the Spirit and keeps right with God is terror to Satan. The very powers of darkness are paralyzed by prayer. It is no wonder that Satan tries to keep our minds fussy in active work till we cannot think in prayer.

Oswald Chambers

Noise and words and frenzied, hectic schedules dull our senses, closing our ears to His still, small voice and making us numb to His touch.

Charles Swindoll

274

EXCUSES DON'T WORK

People's own foolishness ruins their lives, but in their minds they blame the Lord.

Proverbs 19:3 NCV

Excuses are everywhere . . . excellence is not. Whether you're a student in school or a corporate CEO, your work is a picture book of your priorities. So whatever your job description, it's up to you, and no one else, to become masterful at your craft. It's up to you to do your work right, and to do it right now.

Because we humans are such creative excuse-makers, all of the best excuses have already been taken—we've heard them all before.

So if you're wasting your time trying to concoct a new and improved excuse, don't bother. It's impossible. A far better strategy is this: do the work. Now. Then, let your excellent work speak loudly and convincingly for itself.

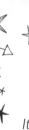

MORE FROM GOD'S WORD

It is God's will that your good lives should silence those who make foolish accusations against you. You are not slaves; you are free. But your freedom is not an excuse to do evil. You are free to live as God's slaves.

1 Peter 2:15-16 NLT

You can be sure that no immoral, impure, or greedy person will inherit the Kingdom of Christ and of God. For a greedy person is really an idolater who worships the things of this world. Don't be fooled by those who try to excuse these sins, for the terrible anger of God comes upon all those who disobey him.

Ephesians 5:5-6 NLT

Let us live in a right way . . . clothe yourselves with the Lord Jesus Christ and forget about satisfying your sinful self.

Romans 13:13-14 NCV

Therefore, get your minds ready for action, being self-disciplined, and set your hope completely on the grace to be brought to you at the revelation of Jesus Christ.

1 Peter 1:13 HCSB

SOME BIG IDEAS

Replace your excuses with fresh determination.

Charles Swindoll

An excuse is only the skin of a reason stuffed with a lie.

Vance Havner

We need to stop focusing on our lacks and stop giving out excuses and start looking at and listening to Jesus.

Anne Graham Lotz

Making up a string of excuses is usually harder than doing the work.

Marie T. Freeman

Today, think of something important that you've been putting off. Then think of the excuses you've used to avoid that responsibility. Finally, ask yourself what you can do today to finish the work you've been avoiding.

YOU NEED THE RIGHT KIND OF FELLOWSHIP

So reach out and welcome one another to God's glory. Jesus did it; now you do it!

Romans 15:7 MSG

If you genuinely want to become the kind of person who experiences a closer relationship with God, you'll need to build closer relationships with godly people. That's why fellowship with like-minded believers should be an integral part of your life. Your association with fellow Christians should be uplifting, enlightening, encouraging, and (above all) consistent.

Are your friends the kind of people who encourage you to seek God's will and to obey God's Word? If so, you've chosen your friends wisely. And that's a good thing because when you choose friends who honor God, you'll find it easier to honor Him, too.

MORE FROM GOD'S WORD

You must get along with each other. You must learn to be considerate of one another, cultivating a life in common.

1 Corinthians 1:10 MSG

Don't you realize that all of you together are the temple of God and that the Spirit of God lives in you?

1 Corinthians 3:16 NLT

Don't become partners with those who reject God. How can you make a partnership out of right and wrong? That's not partnership; that's war. Is light best friends with dark?

2 Corinthians 6:14 MSG

He keeps us in step with each other. His very breath and blood flow through us, nourishing us so that we will grow up healthy in God, robust in love.

Ephesians 4:16 MSG

NEXT

SOME BIG IDEAS

One of the ways God refills us after failure is through the blessing of Christian fellowship. Just experiencing the joy of simple activities shared with other children of God can have a healing effect on us.

Anne Graham Lotz

Brotherly love is still the distinguishing badge of every true Christian.

Matthew Henry

I hope you will find a few folks who walk with God to also walk with you through the seasons of your life.

John Eldredge

Be united with other Christians.
A wall with loose bricks is not good.
The bricks must be cemented together.
Corrie ten Boom

FOCUS ON SPIRITUAL MATTERS

For those whose lives are according to the flesh think about the things of the flesh, but those whose lives are according to the Spirit, about the things of the Spirit.

Romans 8:5 HCSB

Is Christ the focus of your life? Are you fired with enthusiasm for Him? Are you an energized Christian who allows God's Son to reign over every aspect of your day? Make no mistake: that's exactly what God intends for you to do.

God has given you the gift of eternal life through His Son. In response to God's priceless gift, you are instructed to focus your thoughts, your prayers, and your energies upon God and His only begotten Son. To do so, you must resist the subtle yet powerful temptation to become a "spiritual dabbler."

A person who dabbles in the Christian faith is unwilling to place God in His rightful place: above all other things. Resist that temptation; make God the

cornerstone and the touchstone of your life. When you do, He will give you all the strength and wisdom you need to live victoriously for Him.

MORE FROM GOD'S WORD

Let us lay aside every weight and the sin that so easily ensnares us, and run with endurance the race that lies before us, keeping our eyes on Jesus, the source and perfecter of our faith.

Hebrews 12:1-2 HCSB

Give your entire attention to what God is doing right now, and don't get worked up about what may or may not happen tomorrow. God will help you deal with whatever hard things come up when the time comes.

Matthew 6:34 MSG

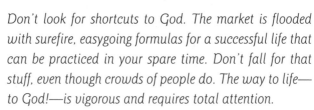

Don't look for shortcuts to God. The market is flooded with surefire, easygoing formulas for a successful life that can be practiced in your spare time. Don't fall for that stuff, even though crowds of people do. The way to life— to God!—is vigorous and requires total attention.

Matthew 7:13-14 MSG

SOME BIG IDEAS

Forgetting your mission leads, inevitably, to getting tangled up in details—details that can take you completely off your path.

Laurie Beth Jones

Paul did one thing. Most of us dabble in forty things. Are you a doer or a dabbler?

Vance Havner

Any thought not centered on God is stolen from Him.

St. John of the Cross

I am convinced beyond a shadow of any doubt that the most valuable pursuit we can embark upon is to know God.

Kay Arthur

How much time do you spend focusing on God and His will for your life? If you answered, "Not much," it's time to reorder your priorities.

DON'T UNDERESTIMATE THE IMPORTANCE OF YOUR FRIENDS

As iron sharpens iron, a friend sharpens a friend.

Proverbs 27:17 NLT

When you hang out with positive people, you feel better about yourself and your world—when you hang out with negative people, you won't. So here's the question: do you want to feel better about yourself and your circumstances . . . or not? The answer you give should help you determine the friends you choose to make—and keep.

If you're really serious about being an optimistic, upbeat, hope-filled Christian, make sure that your friends feel the same way. Because if you choose to hang out with upbeat people, you'll tend to be an upbeat person, too. But if you hang out with the critics, the cynics, and the naysayers, you'll find yourself becoming a cynic, too. And life is far too short for that.

MORE FROM GOD'S WORD

Beloved, if God so loved us, we also ought to love one another.

1 John 4:11 NKJV

This is my command: Love one another the way I loved you. This is the very best way to love. Put your life on the line for your friends.

John 15:12-13 MSG

Finally, all of you be of one mind, having compassion for one another; love as brothers, be tenderhearted, be courteous.

1 Peter 3:8 NKJV

The one who loves his brother remains in the light, and there is no cause for stumbling in him.

1 John 2:10 HCSB

NEXT

YOUR FRIENDS

Take a few minutes to think about your five best
friends. Below write down their names and after
it, a brief reason why they are your friend.

_____

_____

_____

_____

_____

_____

_____

_____

_____

_____

_____

100 ESSENTIAL DEVOS FOR TWEENS

SOME BIG IDEAS

The next best thing to being wise oneself is to live in a circle of those who are.

C. S. Lewis

For better or worse, you will eventually become more and more like the people you associate with. So why not associate with people who make you better, not worse?

Marie T. Freeman

Yes, the Spirit was sent to be our Counselor. Yes, Jesus speaks to us personally. But often he works through another human being.

John Eldredge

> Your friends will have a major impact on your self-image. That's an important reason (but not the only reason) to select your friends carefully.

A friend is one who makes me do my best.

Oswald Chambers

ADDICTIVE SUBSTANCES ARE POISON

Be sober! Be on the alert! Your adversary the Devil is prowling around like a roaring lion, looking for anyone he can devour.

1 Peter 5:8 HCSB

If you'd like a perfect formula for low (or no) self-respect, here it is: get addicted to something that destroys your health or your sanity. If (God forbid) you allow yourself to become addicted, you're steering straight for a boatload of negative consequences, not to mention a big bad dose of negative self-esteem.

Unless you're living on a deserted island, you've heard about people who are full-blown addicts. If you, or someone you love, is suffering from the blight of addiction, remember this: Help is available. Plenty of people have experienced addiction and lived to tell about it . . . so don't give up hope.

And if you're one of those fortunate people who hasn't started experimenting with addictive substances, congratulations! You have just spared yourself a lifetime of headaches and heartaches.

MORE FROM GOD'S WORD

For we do not have a High Priest who cannot sympathize with our weaknesses, but was in all points tempted as we are, yet without sin. Let us therefore come boldly to the throne of grace, that we may obtain mercy and find grace to help in time of need.

Hebrews 4:15-16 NKJV

Jesus responded, "I assure you: Everyone who commits sin is a slave of sin."

John 8:34 HCSB

Death is the reward of an undisciplined life; your foolish decisions trap you in a dead end.

Proverbs 5:23 MSG

SOME BIG IDEAS

One reason I'm a teetotaler is that I got so disgusted being mistreated due to a man's drinking to excess that I never have wanted to run the risk of mistreating my own family by drinking.

Jerry Clower

Warning: addiction and self-esteem can't live for long in the same body.

A man may not be responsible for his last drink, but he certainly was for the first.

Billy Graham

When I feel like circumstances are spiraling downward in my life, God taught me that whether I'm right side up or upside down, I need to turn those circumstances over to Him. He is the only one who can bring balance into my life.

Carole Lewis

The soul that journeys to God, but doesn't shake off its cares and quiet its appetites, is like someone who drags a cart uphill.

St. John of the Cross

SERVE HIM

The greatest among you will be your servant. Whoever exalts himself will be humbled, and whoever humbles himself will be exalted.

Matthew 23:11-12 HCSB

We live in a world that glorifies power, prestige, fame, and money. But the words of Jesus teach us that the most esteemed men and women in this world are not the self-congratulatory leaders of society but are instead the humblest of servants.

Are you willing to become a humble servant for Christ? Are you willing to pitch in and make the world a better place, or are you determined to keep all your blessings to yourself? The answers to these questions will determine the quality and the direction of your day and your life.

Today, you may feel the temptation to take more than you give. You may be tempted to withhold your generosity. Or you may be tempted to build yourself up in the eyes of your friends. Resist those temptations. Instead, serve your friends quietly and without fanfare.

Find a need and fill it . . . humbly. Lend a helping hand . . . anonymously. Share a word of kindness . . . with quiet sincerity. As you go about your daily activities, remember that the Savior of all humanity made Himself a servant, and we, as His followers, must do no less.

MORE FROM GOD'S WORD

So prepare your minds for service and have self-control. All your hope should be for the gift of grace that will be yours when Jesus Christ is shown to you.

1 Peter 1:13 NCV

There are different kinds of gifts, but they are all from the same Spirit. There are different ways to serve but the same Lord to serve.

1 Corinthians 12:4–5 NCV

Therefore, since we receive a kingdom which cannot be shaken, let us show gratitude, by which we may offer to God an acceptable service with reverence and awe....

Hebrews 12:28 NASB

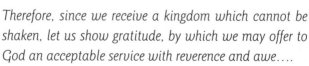

SOME BIG IDEAS

In the very place where God has put us, whatever its limitations, whatever kind of work it may be, we may indeed serve the Lord Christ.

Elisabeth Elliot

God wants us to serve Him with a willing spirit, one that would choose no other way.

Beth Moore

So many times we say that we can't serve God because we aren't whatever is needed. We're not talented enough or smart enough or whatever. But if you are in covenant with Jesus Christ, He is responsible for covering your weaknesses, for being your strength. He will give you His abilities for your disabilities!

Kay Arthur

> Whatever your age, whatever your circumstances, you can serve: Each stage of life's journey is a glorious opportunity to place yourself in the service of the One who is the Giver of all blessings.

Through our service to others, God wants to influence our world for Him.

Vonette Bright

DO FIRST THINGS FIRST

Therefore, get your minds ready for action, being self-disciplined . . . .

1 Peter 1:13 HCSB

"First things first." These words are easy to speak but hard to put into practice. For busy people living in a demanding world, placing first things first can be difficult indeed. Why? Because so many people are expecting so many things from us!

If you're having trouble prioritizing your day, perhaps you've been trying to organize your life according to your own plans, not God's. A better strategy, of course, is to take your daily obligations and place them in the hands of the One who created you. To do so, you must prioritize your day according to God's commandments, and you must seek His will and His wisdom in all matters. Then, you can face the day with the assurance that the same God who created our universe out of nothingness will help you place first things first in your own life.

LOOK

IN

OUT

FOLLOW

Do you feel overwhelmed or confused? Turn the concerns of this day over to God—prayerfully, earnestly, and often. Then, listen for His answer . . . and trust the answer He gives.

MORE FROM GOD'S WORD

Don't abandon wisdom, and she will watch over you; love her, and she will guard you.

Proverbs 4:6 HCSB

And I pray this: that your love will keep on growing in knowledge and every kind of discernment, so that you can determine what really matters and can be pure and blameless in the day of Christ.

Philippians 1:9 HCSB

So teach us to number our days, that we may gain a heart of wisdom.

Psalm 90:12 NKJV

For where your treasure is, there your heart will be also.

Luke 12:34 HCSB

NEXT

SOME BIG IDEAS

Blessed are those who know what on earth they are here on earth to do and set themselves about the business of doing it.

Max Lucado

No test of a man's true character is more conclusive than how he spends his time and his money.

Patrick Morley

> Unless you put first things first, you're bound to finish last. And that means putting God first.

Does God care about all the responsibilities we have to juggle in our daily lives? Of course. But he cares more that our lives demonstrate balance, the ability to discern what is essential and give ourselves fully to it.

Penelope Stokes

The most important business I'm engaged in ought to be the Lord's business. If it ain't, I need to get off and classify myself and see whose side I'm on.

Jerry Clower

TEMPTATIONS ARE EVERYWHERE, AND YOU SHOULD AVOID THEM

Put on the whole armor of God, that you may be able to stand against the wiles of the devil.

Ephesians 6:11 NKJV

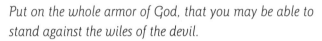

Face facts: you live a temptation-filled world. The devil is hard at work in your neighborhood, and so are his helpers. Here in the 21st century, the bad guys are working around the clock to lead you astray. That's why you must remain vigilant.

In a letter to believers, Peter offers a stern warning: "Your adversary, the devil, prowls around like a roaring lion, seeking someone to devour" (1 Peter 5:8 NASB). What was true in New Testament times is equally true in our own. Satan tempts his prey and then devours them (and it's up to you—and only you—to make sure that you're not one of the ones being devoured!).

ENTER
EXIT

As a believer who seeks a radical relationship with Jesus, you must beware because temptations are everywhere. Satan is determined to win; you must be equally determined that he does not.

MORE FROM GOD'S WORD

But remember that the temptations that come into your life are no different from what others experience. And God is faithful. He will keep the temptation from becoming so strong that you can't stand up against it. When you are tempted, he will show you a way out so that you will not give in to it.

1 Corinthians 10:13 NLT

Be sober, be vigilant; because your adversary the devil walks about like a roaring lion, seeking whom he may devour.

1 Peter 5:8 NKJV

The Lord knows how to deliver the godly out of temptations.

2 Peter 2:9 NKJV

OUT

SOME BIG IDEAS

Jesus faced every temptation known to humanity so that He could identify with us.

Beth Moore

Our battles are first won or lost in the secret places of our will in God's presence, never in full view of the world.

Oswald Chambers

Flee temptation without leaving a forwarding address.

Barbara Johnson

Temptation is not a sin. Even Jesus was tempted. The Lord Jesus gives you the strength needed to resist temptation.

Corrie ten Boom

Temptations are everywhere. It's your job to avoid them . . . or else!

IT PAYS TO FORGIVE

You have heard that it was said, You shall love your neighbor and hate your enemy. But I tell you, love your enemies, and pray for those who persecute you.

Matthew 5:43-44 HCSB

It has been said that life is an exercise in forgiveness. How true. Christ understood the importance of forgiveness when he commanded, "Love your enemies and pray for those who persecute you" (Matthew 5:43-44 NIV). But sometimes, forgiveness is difficult indeed.

When we have been injured or embarrassed, we feel the urge to strike back and to hurt the one who has hurt us. Christ instructs us to do otherwise. Believers are taught that forgiveness is God's way and that mercy is an integral part of God's plan for our lives. In short, we are commanded to weave the thread of forgiveness into the very fabric of our lives.

Today, as you go about your daily affairs, remember that you have already been forgiven by your Heavenly Father, and so, too, should you forgive others. If you

bear bitterness against anyone, take your bitterness to God and leave it there. If you are angry, pray for God's healing hand to calm your spirit. If you are troubled by some past injustice, read God's Word and remember His commandment to forgive. When you follow that commandment and sincerely forgive those who have hurt you, you'll discover that a heavy burden has been lifted from your shoulders. And, you'll discover that although forgiveness is indeed difficult, with God's help, all things are possible.

Learning how to forgive and forget is one of the secrets of a happy Christian life.
Warren Wiersbe

NEXT

FORGIVE AND FORGET

Do you have someone you need to forgive? Write that person's name in one of the boxes below. Then ask God to give you the strength to forgive them.

OUT

MORE FROM GOD'S WORD

Be even-tempered, content with second place, quick to forgive an offense. Forgive as quickly and completely as the Master forgave you. And regardless of what else you put on, wear love. It's your basic, all-purpose garment. Never be without it.

Colossians 3:13-14 MSG

Hatred stirs up trouble, but love forgives all wrongs.

Proverbs 10:12 NCV

Our Father is kind; you be kind. "Don't pick on people, jump on their failures, criticize their faults—unless, of course, you want the same treatment. Don't condemn those who are down; that hardness can boomerang. Be easy on people; you'll find life a lot easier."

Luke 6:36-37 MSG

Be gentle with one another, sensitive. Forgive one another as quickly and thoroughly as God in Christ forgave you.

Ephesians 4:32 MSG

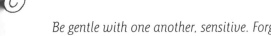

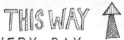
SOME BIG IDEAS

The fact is, God no longer deals with us in judgment but in mercy. If people got what they deserved, this old planet would have ripped apart at the seams centuries ago. Praise God that because of His great love "we are not consumed, for his compassions never fail" (Lam. 3:22).

Joni Eareckson Tada

When God forgives, He forgets. He buries our sins in the sea and puts a sign on the shore saying, "No Fishing Allowed."

Corrie ten Boom

Our forgiveness toward others should flow from a realization and appreciation of God's forgiveness toward us.

Franklin Graham

Holding a grudge? Drop it. Never expect other people to be more forgiving than you are. And remember: the best time to forgive is now.

DEVO 96

SILENCE IS INDEED GOLDEN

Be silent before the Lord and wait expectantly for Him.

Psalm 37:7 HCSB

When you have doubts, remember this: God isn't on a coffee break, and He hasn't moved out of town. God isn't taking a long vacation, and He isn't snoozing on the couch. He's right here, right now, listening to your thoughts and prayers, watching over your every move.

The Bible teaches that a wonderful way to get to know God is simply to be still and listen to Him. But sometimes, you may find it hard to slow down and listen. As the demands of everyday life weigh down upon you, you may be tempted to ignore God's presence or—worse yet—to rebel against His commandments. But, when you quiet yourself and acknowledge His presence, God touches your heart and restores your spirits. So why not let Him do it right now? If you really want to know Him better, silence is a wonderful place to start.

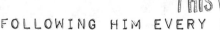 
MORE FROM GOD'S WORD

Be still, and know that I am God.

Psalm 46:10 NKJV

In quietness and confidence shall be your strength.

Isaiah 30:15 NKJV

I am not alone, because the Father is with Me.

John 16:32 HCSB

Draw near to God, and He will draw near to you.

James 4:8 HCSB

You live in a noisy world filled with distractions, a world where silence is in short supply. But God wants you to carve out quiet moments with Him. Silence is, indeed, golden.

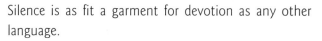

Growth takes place in quietness, in hidden ways, in silence and solitude. The process is not accessible to observation.

Eugene Peterson

Silence is as fit a garment for devotion as any other language.

C. H. Spurgeon

If you, too, will learn to wait upon God, to get alone with Him, and remain silent so that you can hear His voice when He is ready to speak to you, what a difference it will make in your life!

Kay Arthur

There are times when to speak is to violate the moment—when silence represents the highest respect. The word for such times is reverence.

Max Lucado

HAVE A HEALTHY FEAR OF GOD

Since we are receiving a Kingdom that cannot be destroyed, let us be thankful and please God by worshiping him with holy fear and awe.

Hebrews 12:28 NLT

D o you possess a healthy, fearful respect for God's power? Hopefully so. After all, the lesson from the Book of Proverbs is clear: "The fear of the Lord is the beginning of knowledge, but fools despise wisdom and instruction" (1:7 NKJV). Yet, you live in a world that often ignores the role that God plays in shaping the affairs of mankind. You live in a world where too many people consider it "unfashionable" or "unseemly" to discuss the fear of God. Don't count yourself among their number.

God maintains absolute sovereignty over His creation, and His power is beyond comprehension. As believers, we must cultivate a sincere respect for God's awesome power. The fear of the Lord is, indeed, the

beginning of knowledge. So today, as you face the realities of everyday life, remember this: until you acquire a healthy, respectful fear of God's power, your education is incomplete, and so is your faith.

MORE FROM GOD'S WORD

The fear of the Lord is the beginning of knowledge, but fools despise wisdom and discipline.

Proverbs 1:7 NIV

Honor all people. Love the brotherhood. Fear God. Honor the king.

1 Peter 2:17 NKJV

Fear the LORD your God, serve him only and take your oaths in his name.

Deuteronomy 6:13 NIV

Don't consider yourself to be wise; fear the Lord and turn away from evil.

Proverbs 3:7 HCSB

NEXT

SOME BIG IDEAS

When true believers are awed by the greatness of God and by the privilege of becoming His children, then they become sincerely motivated, effective evangelists.

Bill Hybels

> It's the right kind of fear: Your respect for God should make you fearful of disobeying Him . . . very fearful.

A healthy fear of God will do much to deter us from sin.

Charles Swindoll

The fear of God is the death of every other fear.

C. H. Spurgeon

The remarkable thing about fearing God is that when you fear God, you fear nothing else, whereas if you do not fear God, you fear everything else.

Oswald Chambers

SIN EQUALS DISASTER

Jesus responded, "I assure you: Everyone who commits sin is a slave of sin."

John 8:34 HCSB

ecause we are creatures of free will, we may disobey God whenever we choose. But when we do so, we put ourselves and our loved ones in peril. Why? Because disobedience invites disaster. We cannot sin against God without consequences. We cannot live outside His will without injury. We cannot distance ourselves from God without hardening our hearts. We cannot yield to the ever-tempting distractions of our world and, at the same time, enjoy God's peace.

Sometimes, in a futile attempt to justify our behaviors, we make a distinction between "big" sins and "little" ones. To do so is a mistake of "big" proportions. Sins of all shapes and sizes have the power to do us great harm. And in a world where sin is big business, that's certainly a sobering thought.

ENTER
EXIT

MORE FROM GOD'S WORD

But now being made free from sin, and become servants to God, ye have your fruit unto holiness, and the end everlasting life. For the wages of sin is death; but the gift of God is eternal life through Jesus Christ our Lord.

Romans 6:22-23 KJV

For all have sinned and fall short of the glory of God.

Romans 3:23 HCSB

Disaster pursues sinners, but good rewards the righteous.

Proverbs 13:21 HCSB

The one who conceals his sins will not prosper, but whoever confesses and renounces them will find mercy.

Proverbs 28:13 HCSB

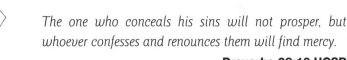

SOME BIG IDEAS

Before we can be filled with the Living Water, we must be cleansed of sin. Before we can be cleansed of sin, we must be convicted. And sometimes it's painful. And shameful.

Anne Graham Lotz

We cannot out-sin God's ability to forgive us.

Beth Moore

He loved us even while we were yet sinners at war with Him!

Bill Bright

There's none so blind as those who will not see.

Matthew Henry

Sometimes immorality is obvious and sometimes it's not. So beware: the most subtle forms of sin are often the most dangerous.

SHARE YOUR FAITH

And I say to you, anyone who acknowledges Me before men, the Son of Man will also acknowledge him before the angels of God; but whoever denies Me before men will be denied before the angels of God.

Luke 12:8-9 HCSB

Let's get one thing straight: those of us who are Christians should be willing to talk about the things that Christ has done for us. Our personal testimonies are vitally important, but sometimes, because of shyness or insecurities, we're afraid to share our experiences. And that's unfortunate.

We live in a world that desperately needs the healing message of Jesus. Every believer, each in their own way, bears responsibility for sharing the Good News of our Savior. And it is important to remember that we bear testimony through both words and actions.

If you seek to be a radical follower of Christ, then it's time for you to share your testimony with others. So today, preach the Gospel through your words and your deeds . . . but not necessarily in that order.

But sanctify the Lord God in your hearts, and always be ready to give a defense to everyone who asks you a reason for the hope that is in you.

1 Peter 3:15 HCSB

You are the light of the world. A city that is set on a hill cannot be hidden. Nor do they light a lamp and put it under a basket, but on a lampstand, and it gives light to all who are in the house. Let your light so shine before men, that they may see your good works and glorify your Father in heaven.

Matthew 5:14–16 NKJV

Whatever I tell you in the dark, speak in the light; and what you hear in the ear, preach on the housetops.

Matthew 10:27 NKJV

And I say to you, anyone who acknowledges Me before men, the Son of Man will also acknowledge him before the angels of God; but whoever denies Me before men will be denied before the angels of God.

Luke 12:8-9 HCSB

NEXT

SOME BIG IDEAS

To take up the cross means that you take your stand for the Lord Jesus no matter what it costs.

Billy Graham

Usually it is those who know Him that bring Him to others. That is why the Church, the whole body of Christians showing Him to one another, is so important.

C. S. Lewis

If your eternity with God is secure (because you believe in Jesus), you have a profound responsibility to tell as many people as you can about the eternal life that Christ offers to those who believe in Him.

Our Lord is searching for people who will make a difference. Christians dare not dissolve into the background or blend into the neutral scenery of the world.

Charles Swindoll

The sermon of your life in tough times ministers to people more powerfully than the most eloquent speaker.

Bill Bright

THE ULTIMATE CHOICE

For God so loved the world that He gave His only begotten Son, that whoever believes in Him should not perish but have everlasting life.

John 3:16 NKJV

Your ability to envision the future, like your life here on earth, is limited. God's vision, however, is not burdened by any such limitations. He sees all things, He knows all things, and His plans for you extend throughout eternity.

God's plans are not limited to the events of daily life. Your Heavenly Father has bigger things in mind for you . . . much bigger things. So praise the Creator for the gift of eternal life and share the Good News with all who cross your path. And remember: if you have given your heart to the Son, you belong to the Father—today, tomorrow, and for all eternity.

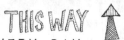

MORE FROM GOD'S WORD

And this is the testimony: God has given us eternal life, and this life is in His Son. The one who has the Son has life. The one who doesn't have the Son of God does not have life. I have written these things to you who believe in the name of the Son of God, so that you may know that you have eternal life.

1 John 5:11-13 HCSB

Pursue righteousness, godliness, faith, love, endurance, and gentleness. Fight the good fight for the faith; take hold of eternal life, to which you were called and have made a good confession before many witnesses.

1 Timothy 6:11-12 HCSB

Jesus said to her, "I am the resurrection and the life. The one who believes in Me, even if he dies, will live. Everyone who lives and believes in Me will never die—ever. Do you believe this?"

John 11:25-26 HCSB

OUT

SOME BIG IDEAS

God loves you and wants you to experience peace and life—abundant and eternal.

Billy Graham

If you are a believer, your judgment will not determine your eternal destiny. Christ's finished work on Calvary was applied to you the moment you accepted Christ as Savior.

Beth Moore

Those of us who know the wonderful grace of redemption look forward to an eternity with God, when all things will be made new, when all our longings will at last find ultimate and final satisfaction.

Joseph Stowell

> The ultimate choice for you is the choice to invite God's Son into your heart. Choose wisely . . . and immediately.

Once a man is united to God, how could he not live forever? Once a man is separated from God, what can he do but wither and die?

C. S. Lewis

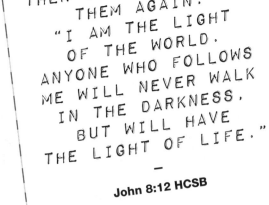

THEN JESUS SPOKE TO
THEM AGAIN:
"I AM THE LIGHT
OF THE WORLD.
ANYONE WHO FOLLOWS
ME WILL NEVER WALK
IN THE DARKNESS,
BUT WILL HAVE
THE LIGHT OF LIFE."

—

John 8:12 HCSB

OUT